HOW TO AVOID QUITTING

HOW TO AVOID QUITTING

Steps to Staying in the Game of Life

Earl Dixon

How to Avoid Quitting

Copyright © 2018 Earl Dixon

All rights reserved.
No part of this book may be reproduced or transmitted in any form or by any means, electronic or mechanically, including photocopying, recording, or by any information storage or retrieval system, without the express written permission of the author except where permitted by law or for the use of brief quotations in a book review or scholarly journal. Your support of the author's rights is appreciated.

ISBN 978-0-9713927-3-1

Cover design by Brand It Beautifully™
www.branditbeautifully.com

Editing
Mequille Jones, Kimberly Walker Williams,
Eboni Vasser, Jessie McLemore

To contact Earl Dixon
http://www.edjministries.org/

CONTENTS

SPECIAL THANKS 1
PREFACE 3
INTRODUCTION 7
CHAPTER 1 TAKE SUICIDE OFF THE TABLE 9
CHAPTER 2 KNOW THAT GOD IS WITH YOU 21
CHAPTER 3 STAND ON GOD'S WORD 29
CHAPTER 4 GET IN FAITH 35
CHAPTER 5 LET GO OF BITTERNESS! 41
CHAPTER 6 KILL ENTITLEMENT 47
CHAPTER 7 AVOID MAKING DESPERATE MOVES ... 51
CHAPTER 8 GET A NEW STRATEGY 59
CHAPTER 9 EMBRACE ISOLATION 63
CHAPTER 10 BELIEVE FOR MIRACLES BUT WORK PRINCIPLES 69
CHAPTER 11 MAKE UGLY LOOK GOOD 73
CHAPTER 12 PRAY FOR A MARY & MARTHA 81
CHAPTER 13 MAKE REST A PRIORITY 89
CHAPTER 14 PUT YOUR DEVELOPMENT OVER YOUR REPUTATION 99
CHAPTER 15 FORGIVE 105
APPENDIX THE ANSWER SHEET: STARTER KIT 111

SPECIAL THANKS

I would like to thank my wife and ministry partner for the last 30 years, **Mrs. Pamela A. Dixon,** for your UNCOMPROMISING COMMITMENT to our marriage, family, and ministry. Through the years, I have witnessed many women leave and divorce their husbands for just a few of the things you have endured. You demonstrate a relentless dedication to our covenant of marriage and ministry. **Thank you.**

To my children **Ashley, Gabriel & Jonathon:** Let me apologize for the negative experiences you have withstood, as a result of decisions I made as your father. I also recognize the pains you bore, due to my service to God's people. For this I apologize and I thank you for your unconditional love through it all.

Bishop Theo & Dr. Florence Bailey: You extended a lifeline to my family and I when we were drowning. I would like to simply say, "Thank you". I will discuss the many situations of how your presence ministered to my family and I, during a very challenging time in our lives.

Pastor Gary Cooper and Pastor Lorenzo Huggins: Your ears should be healed by now after listening to me for many hours and days. Thank you both for being a sounding board in my life many times.

Bishop Steven A. Davis and the *New Birth Birmingham Family.* You have no clue of the magnitude your ministry served in one of the most trying times of my life! For months you all were a breath of FRESH air!

Min. Christopher Walker, God used you in a major way to bring me back to a LIFE of FAITH and TRUST in HIM! Thank you for all you have done.

Valencia Carpenter, Thank you for helping to bring healing to the little boy in North Birmingham. You blessed me more than you'll ever no.

To the REMAINING members of Life Changers Ministries International/Kingdom Ministries: "THANK YOU!" Your commitment to remain in our lives during personal struggles and numerous ministry failures have ministered to me tremendously. Despite the countless negative commentaries, you continue to allow me the precious opportunity to minister God's word to you and for that I thank you. My family and I will forever cherish your love and support.

Special thanks to Lady Cecily Holt and Min. Latonya Seals along with your families! Your honor and respect spoke to me more than any seed you've ever sown in our lives and ministry. You ladies are a testimony of how leadership should be honored.

Lastly, to every person that has shown us acts of kindness to which I did not name, I thank you immensely.

PREFACE

If there was ever one thing that I am guilty of, it's going too far in explaining or trying to be clear on a subject.

Frequently in ministry and life, I've had people tell me to stop apologizing. But in my head, I wasn't saying I'm sorry, I was only trying to be clear as it related to the matter at hand.

In my preface, I want to be perfectly clear on the purpose and intent of this book.

Although brief in volume, this book has taken me years to complete. Previously, I wanted to give a very real and raw picture of MY SIDE of an ugly situation. An ugly situation which *(in my opinion)* launched some of the most horrific, embarrassing, and painful times for me as well as my family.

My plan was to use this publication as a way of finally telling my side of what happened. My desire was to clarify the series of events, which resulted in a foul separation. This separation caused me to make a decision to resign from a ministry, in which I served faithfully for over fourteen (14) years. I needed to write about all of the appalling things that church members, family, and so called good friends had done to my family and I. These negative deeds contributed to the years of pain and suffering we endured. But through God, we eventually overcame.

I began writing chapter after chapter. I describe some of the terrible things we've experienced. Then one day it finally hit me, I started to realize why writing this book was so difficult. It was because God almighty had other plans. God wanted me to share, but not in the way that I would have desired.

For years, my family and I dealt with what others said happened. But in my opinion, we never really got to tell our side of it.

I will never forget the day a real release took place in my life and the direction of this book. I was riding and I heard God say these words, **"Your level of breakthrough will be decided by your lack or unwillingness to tell your side."** God continued to speak to me and said, **"The barometer to use in determining your level of healing is in your lack of desire to tell your side."** God further said, **"When your desire to tell your side is no longer relevant or important, that's when you will know you are healed; you are over it and over people!"**

Right then and there I let it all go! It was at that moment I realized that my side of the story didn't matter. All I needed to focus on in this book was what my family and I did to overcome. I needed to share with God's people how we overcame loss, disappointment, betrayal, and the things I did, which caused years of pain.

This book will detail some of THE MOST embarrassing situations I've ever experienced in my lifetime. Again, I need to clarify five (5) things and they are as follows:

1. This is not an attempt tell my side of a story that has already been told.
2. This is not an attempt to rehash any hurt of any person(s) involved.
3. This is not a way to vindicate myself *(God has already done that)*.

4. This is not me seeking ANYONE'S approval *(God has already done that)*.
5. These are not the words of an angry man seeking revenge or to intentionally hurt anyone. On the contrary, after fifteen (15) years, my goal is to forget all offenses and to be reconciled. Simply stated, just let bygones be bygones.

This book is also for that pastor, minister, deacon, church member and/or person in general, which did or was accused of doing something that was deemed so appalling that they have decided to abandon ministry and at times, life. This book is for that person that has crawled in a HOLE of SHAME, declaring that life for them will never be close to what it was. This book is for ANYONE who has committed a shameful crime or act and is allowing the insulting opinions of others to keep them from experiencing the restoration power of a graceful, merciful, loving, and forgiving God!

Therefore, if you know of anyone who has parked their lives on the side of the road, vowing never to drive again; do them a favor, and purchase them a copy of this book. It will be the gasoline they need to fuel their faith and continue on their journey to a great life in God!

Earl Dixon

INTRODUCTION

I will be the first to tell you that I know well, the pain of family & ministry betrayals; loss of friendships; the embarrassment of automobile repossessions; utilities being disconnected; bankruptcies; pawning personal items; getting food stamps from church members just to eat, and any other life disappointments that one could have possibly experienced while enduring a major setback.

As you read this book, focus on what we did to overcome some of these very challenging situations in our lives. I truly believe that God has restored and raised me up for such a time as this. I feel compelled to make evident to anyone who has or is currently suffering from a life disappointment, that they can rebound and use their situation to help someone else.

In fact, over the years, my wife and I often refer to ourselves as the poster children for how to make ugly look really good! We know well how to make your mess your message. Just as it was a blessing for me to write this, I truly hope this book blesses you as you read it!

CHAPTER 1

TAKE SUICIDE OFF THE TABLE

Wait, before you bypass this chapter with the thought of… *"I don't need this chapter!"* You or somebody you know does need to understand how to take suicide off the table. Not only am I going to talk to you about how I had constant thoughts of suicide, but I will also reveal what I believe triggered or encouraged those thoughts of taking my own life, literally every day! However, before I do that, let's examine an epidemic that is increasing at an alarming rate in America.

According to research released by the National Alliance of Mental Illness (NAMI), I discovered some very disturbing information concerning mental illness in the African American Community. NAMI suggests that African Americans are no different when it comes to prevalence of mental health conditions, when compared to the rest of the population. However, your concerns or experiences and how you understand and cope with these conditions may be different *(cited from https://www.nami.org/find-support/diverse-communities/african-americans)*.

Why Does Mental Health Matter?

It matters because mental health is a real part of our total body's health/well-being. For years I had my own private mental struggles. These mental struggles often led me to experience feelings of deep depression. Yes, I was anointed, appointed and preaching the gospel of Jesus Christ, while simultaneously wrestling at night in my head. Wrestling with the constant thought of taking my own life!

What I discovered in the long run was without mental health, one cannot be completely healthy. According to NAMI, any part of the body—including the brain—can get sick. We all experience emotional ups and downs from time to time caused by events in our lives. Mental health conditions go beyond these emotional reactions to specific situations. They are medical conditions that cause changes in how we think and feel and in our mood. These changes can alter your life because they make it hard to relate to others and function the way you used to *(cite from https://www.nami.org/find-support/diverse-communities/african-americans)*.

For me, my unhealthy mental state originated in my childhood. I was a hurt little boy, who grew up in a home in which I despised with a passion. No one really knew it at that time because we didn't discuss things of that nature. But I can truly say I HATED my environment.

When I was a young man, I went to a school where kids fought a lot! Although my family had a reputation that demanded no one challenge or fought me, I still hated seeing other children (bullies) walk up to a good kid, who was just trying to get an education, and would slap the kid down to the ground for no apparent reason. No one ever knew this, but I remember seeing a young boy lying dead in our elementary school from a stab wound. Seeing that boy lying dead in our school did something to me mentally. But because of the environment I was in, if I showed any signs of fear, it would easily make me a target for being bullied as well. So I said nothing and internalized those feelings for years.

I could literally write a book on just the horrific things I saw as a child that were traumatizing. Even in my adult life, I always felt like I was continuously misunderstood. Whenever I tried to express how various traumatic events I witnessed negatively affected me, I sensed from my family members that it was always misinterpreted. They would assume that I was implying that either they, or my mom, were bad people. All I was saying was, some of those incidents scared the hell out of me, many of which I believe traumatized me as well.

I can remember a fight between my mom and stepfather, which involved both having guns. I recall standing between them both and one of the guns went off! My mom was shot by my step-father and there I was, not even fifteen (15) years of age, completely traumatized after witnessing this incident! Then get this, no one ever thought to check to see how I was doing or what this could have done to me psychologically! For years we (the children in the family) were exposed to all types of guns. But secretly, I was literally gun shy. So much so, I couldn't stand to hear the sound of a firecracker. For years, I continued to go to one 4th of July gathering after another, with a silent fear of these loud sounds! My environment and ignorance wouldn't allow me to simply say, *"I'm afraid."*

As a result, years later while saved, in the church, and preaching the gospel of Jesus Christ, I was able to release those fears. I did this through the Word of God found in **2 Timothy 1:7**, which states, *"For God hath not given us the spirit of fear; but of power, and of love, and of a sound mind (King James Version)."*

Although I had conquered the fear, every time I wanted to express what and how this environment impacted me, my family would translate it as me saying, "my mom was bad" or "I didn't like my family," which was not all true. In my mind, ALL I was saying is that these *negative* events, circumstances, and situations *positively* affected me. I say positively because they made me desire to be the total opposite of all the negatives I had been exposed to. However, on the other hand, I didn't realize I hated these experiences so much, until they gave me an unhealthy drive and push to be successful. It was unhealthy because it drove me to push myself and everything around me unrealistically at times. This unhealthy appetite for success caused me to privately live a life through ministry & my children that I felt was ripped from me. But every time I made an attempt to articulate these traumas, all I got was… "Man that was years ago, you should be over that by now, your life wasn't that bad! Your mom did the best she could." Even as I write this book, I'm saying to myself, "Could you all not see?" What I said wasn't about YOU, it was about ME! Much of my family and others just happen to be in the picture! It was never a knock against my mom! My mom was an incredibly awesome woman who I learned so much from.

Nonetheless, it was an environment that would not give me the freedom to express my inner fears. Thereby, causing some mental challenges do to the internalization of negative thoughts and feelings. Thoughts and feelings that should have been dealt with years before I became an adult. I had a big mouth on one end, coupled with several internalizing mental views which often caused me to entertain the actual thought of suicide!

So what does this have to do with taking suicide off the table? You see, for years, success for me wasn't a goal or aspiration. Success became a silent obsession, with being totally opposite of what I saw because I literally hated my past environment. I was obsessed with starting a legacy of my own; something totally different from my opinion of my broken and dysfunctional parental heritage. As time passed, I discovered most of what I thought was the problem, really wasn't the problem. My problem was MEDICAL! Yes, I said it! Through research and newfound knowledge, I learned to accept the fact that my mental challenges stemmed from the internalization of my traumatic childhood.

Although I never used any medication to treat my mental pains, I do urge any person who feels that what you are suffering from is deeper than some personal experiences to please seek medical advice from a licensed professional. If you do not have the spiritual information or spiritual fortitude to overcome, I would strongly suggest that you go to a doctor soon. That being said, I know I've defeated the spirit of depression using biblical principles that I found in the Word of God!

Keep reading this book and I will tell you how I overcame it. I started this book here because mental health and suicide is rising at a rapid rate in America. If you feel you or a loved one might be experiencing a mental health condition that is causing depression or thoughts of suicide, please seek spiritual and medical help immediately!

These can also be biological brain disorders. Anyone can develop a mental health problem. In a lot of instances, it isn't your fault or your family's fault.

African Americans sometimes experience more severe forms of mental health conditions due to unmet needs and other barriers. According to the *Health and Human Services Office of Minority Health*, African Americans are 20% more likely to experience serious mental health problems than the general population. Common mental health disorders among African Americans include:

- Major depression.
- Attention deficit hyperactivity disorder (ADHD).
- Suicide, among young African American men.
- Post-traumatic Stress Disorder (PTSD), because African Americans are more likely to be victims of violent crime.

African Americans are also more likely to experience certain factors that increase the risk for developing a mental health condition:

- **Homelessness.** People experiencing homelessness are at a greater risk of developing a mental health condition. African Americans make up 40% of the homeless population.
- **Exposure to violence** increases the risk of developing a mental health condition such as depression, anxiety and post-traumatic stress disorder.

How To Avoid Quitting

African American children are more likely to be exposed to violence than other children.

In the African American community, many people misunderstand what a mental health condition is and don't talk about this topic. This lack of knowledge leads many to believe that a mental health condition is a personal weakness or some sort of punishment from God. African Americans may be reluctant to discuss mental health issues and seek treatment because of the shame and stigma associated with such conditions *(cited from https://www.nami.org/find-support/diverse-communities/african-americans and https://minorityhealth.hhs.gov/omh/browse.aspx?lvl=4&lvlid=24)*.

Due to my own ignorance, for years I dealt with this in silence. Moreover, after accepting the call to ministry and ultimately becoming a Pastor, that painful silence greatly increased. There was no way I would utter such words from my mouth because my ignorance at that time led me to believe that I would be admitting to being weak and faithless. Many African Americans have trouble recognizing the signs and symptoms of mental health conditions, leading to underestimating the effects and impact of mental health conditions. Some may think of depression as "the blues" or something to "snap out of."

Don't let fear of what others may think, prevent you or a loved one from getting the help they desperately need. One (1) in five (5) people are affected by mental illness *(cited from http://www.mentalhealthamerica.net/issues/state-mental-health-america)*. This means even if we don't talk about it, more than likely we have one of these illnesses and/or know someone who does.

If reading this book is your attempt to overcome a traumatic setback, let me be the first to tell you, it will NEVER happen as long as suicide is a constant thought or option in your mind! If you are going to get mentally healthy, you must first take the option of suicide off the table!

So here I am saved, love God, and thought I had done a pretty decent job of developing a good life. I have a wife, three (3) children, and ministry. God had given me so many reasons to celebrate. But, I would still experience moments where I would be sad when nothing was wrong. Then at times, I'd get this thought that said, "Just kill yourself." As a preacher for over thirty (30) years, in an environment that trains people how to cast down imaginations (NOT OUT BUT DOWN), by bringing thoughts into CAPITIVITY, and to the OBEDIENCE of Christ! I later discovered that the casting down of thoughts now implies that these thoughts will NEVER go away. These thoughts will always be there. We just have to learn how to boldly bring these thoughts into the subjection and the obedience of Christ. As I stated in my preface and introduction, the purpose of this book is to talk more about what I did to rebound and overcome several years of traumatic and horrific life experiences. That being said, without name dropping or getting too specific; I am trying to do what I believe in my heart God has instructed me to do when a snowball of horrible events started happening in my life!

A church that I pastored for years brought some very ugly accusations against me. Many people say they didn't, but I witnessed first-hand many people who literally withdrew from me. Family and friends alike said things that led me to believe that they actually believed all of the negative things that people were saying about me. Not to mention I had some personal struggles of my own, which led to me filing chapter seven (7) bankruptcy. I lost four (4) cars to repossession, *(one while preaching at church)*. I had to move two (2) times to avoid evictions or foreclosures, while at the same time preaching to people whom I will NEVER forget. Although many left the church, in the midst of it all, a faithful few kept showing up and allowing me to minister the goodness of Jesus Christ in their lives!

After all these years, yet another traumatic situation to endure. I'm almost fifty (50) years old and I found myself living upstairs, in my church, with my wife, and three (3) children. For years, I've been moving forward in my childhood aspirations. But, now I'm at a brick wall that I can't seem to get down. Every day I'm struggling! But like the little boy in North Birmingham who couldn't vocalize what he was feeling, I am now a grown man, husband, daddy, and pastor who has to internalize every fear I was feeling.

Then, to add insult to injury, people didn't help make it any better. Again, without calling names, here are some of the things that happened:

- One day I ran into someone who I legitimately owed money to. I know they meant well, but their response to me was, "Hey there… I heard you are going through really bad. I know you owe me, but don't worry about that right now. I heard you are bleeding bad… Just stop your bleeding!"
- There was another occasion where a preacher said, "Man… I told God to bless you because when your life lines up with your preaching, you are going to be something else!" I was like really?

- But the one that really got me was when I was in a local grocery store. An elderly woman who knew me from our TV ministry said out loud in the store, "Hey pastor… they saying you left that church. Took members and stole all the money… but baby I know better than that. You would never do that!" Although she may not have believed it, she spoke so loud that others were given the opportunity to judge me, while I stood there and listened. It was so embarrassing!
- Then one day I was eating lunch with a very prominent pastor. I know he was trying to encourage me but he said, Earl be encouraged. The preachers are laughing at you man, but just stay focused and keep obeying God. I'm like, "Wow!" Thanks for letting me know I'm being laughed at. And not to mention by people who should have been praying for me at that!

At this point I'm going… *"Wow God, what on earth are people saying about me?"* One day, after thoughts of suicide for years, I decided, "God, this isn't fair." I concluded that I wanted to check out. Still, anyone who knows me knows I love my family and although I felt I was ready to leave them, my concern was that I didn't want them to suffer any more than what they had already suffered. Taking a gun and getting it done was NEVER an option. I wanted to die though, but I needed to make it look like an accident. This way my wife and kids would at least be able to cash in the insurance policies I had at the time.

As a result, I decided I'd go to the lake and float way out on the water. I was really going to make it look like a boating accident. That way, they would be able to cash in, not having to worry about my death, and having enough provision to live off of. So, I head to the lake to get a boat. I've been going to this lake for years, but this time I intentionally went to a place that I had never fished before. Suddenly, I hear a voice with such clarity say, *"Throw your line."* I obeyed and threw my line. It was as if I threw the bait right into a fish's mouth! I ended up catching a nice fish too. Now my fishing instincts kick in. I stayed on that lake and fished a few hours. Consequently, I caught one of the largest amount of fish I had ever caught and suicide was never a thought in mind the entire time on that water! This experience is why I'll be writing another book entitled *The Fish That Saved My Life!* God really looked out for me that day. I've suffered many trying times since that day on the lake. However, suicide is NEVER and will never ever be an option for me!

If you are reading this book and deal with constant thoughts of suicide, let's be bold and cancel them today, for real. Why? Because God wanted me to share my story so you too, can take that option off the table. Regardless of how hard life or your situation is, suicide is never an option on the table of life.

NOTE: If my story wasn't enough, I challenge you to read this book in its entirety. PLEASE seek medical help if needed! By all means, read and reread the information I gave on what I did to overcome the spirit of depression in this book. It will help you win.

Earl Dixon

CHAPTER 2

KNOW THAT GOD IS WITH YOU

Isaiah 43:2 (NLT)" *² When you go through deep waters, I will be with you. When you go through rivers of difficulty, you will not drown. When you walk through the fire of oppression, you will not be burned up; the flames will not consume you.*

When many of us face overwhelming situations, we often believe God isn't there or not concerned. This is simply not true, especially for those who have accepted Jesus Christ as your personal Lord and Savior! Frequently, it's satan's plan to get us so focused on what we're going through, that we're unable to recognize God's presence in the midst.

Although I know **I Corinthians 10:13-14** states, *"¹³ The temptations in your life are no different from what others experience. And God is faithful. He will not allow the temptation to be more than you can stand. When you are tempted, he will show you a way out so that you can endure."* I must admit, there was a time when it appeared that we were alone. This is why we all need biblical convictions from God's Word as reassurance in our most adverse situations. Then we can be certain that God is with us.

I don't care what you are rebounding from, I promise you, if you get a revelation of God's presence in your life, you will be amazed as to how you will approach your current situation differently than times before.

I will never forget the countless days of anxiety and depression I felt, while dealing with all that mess. I had consistent headaches, body aches, and ALL the common physicals symptoms associated with anxiety and depression. Simultaneously, my outside appearance reflected a picture of how to go through, while on the inside I was hurting bad!

One day, I was watching Dr. Bridgett Hilliard of Houston, Texas on the television. In this particular segment of the program, she was ministering about how she overcame a terrible church situation that they endured. She went on to talk about how Dr. I.V. Hilliard (her husband) was arrested on a Sunday morning in the pulpit of their church. Dr. Hilliard discussed how bitter she was until one day she began pleading the blood of Jesus over her mind. I concluded, if God could do it for Dr. Hilliard, He definitely could do it for me!

From that point on, every day, I would plead the blood of Jesus over my mind. Consequently, the anxiety and depression left me, but the spirit of fear lingered and became a serious stronghold on me as well.

Satan was determined to keep me captive and not allow me to be totally free. It was as though I could hear voices in my head saying, "you are done, you are finished, and you will never be able to minister in this city again!" One day I literally heard Satan's voice say, "I am going to use this to kill everything you represent in the kingdom of God."

How To Avoid Quitting

It was then that I decided to talk back to Satan just as Jesus did in **Matthew. 4:1-10** (KJV). The scripture teaches us that Jesus spoke back to Satan boldly. It says,

"4 Then was Jesus led up of the Spirit into the wilderness to be tempted of the devil. ²And when he had fasted forty days and forty nights, he was afterward an hungred. ³And when the tempter came to him, he said, If thou be the Son of God, command that these stones be made bread. ⁴But he answered and said, It is written, Man shall not live by bread alone, but by every word that proceedeth out of the mouth of God. ⁵Then the devil taketh him up into the holy city, and setteth him on a pinnacle of the temple, ⁶And saith unto him, If thou be the Son of God, cast thyself down: for it is written, He shall give his angels charge concerning thee: and in their hands they shall bear thee up, lest at any time thou dash thy foot against a stone. ⁷Jesus said unto him, It is written again, Thou shalt not tempt the Lord thy God. ⁸Again, the devil taketh him up into an exceeding high mountain, and sheweth him all the kingdoms of the world, and the glory of them; ⁹And saith unto him, All these things will I give thee, if thou wilt fall down and worship me. ¹⁰Then saith Jesus unto him, Get thee hence, Satan: for it is written, Thou shalt worship the Lord thy God, and him only shalt thou serve."

In Jesus' encounter with Satan, He used the word by saying *"it is written."* It was at this point that all of my faith teaching and training was reignited. I recognized that if I were fearing man, then I needed to find every scripture I could read, meditate on, and confess over my life every day to overcome! God led me right where I needed to be in the Word and boy… did I find some scriptures that spoke directly to the spirit of fear! I encourage you to read and meditate on these powerful scriptures to overcome the spirit of fear in your life:

- **Nahum 1:7** - *"The LORD is good, a strong hold in the day of trouble; and he knoweth them that trust in him."*

- ***Psalms 118:6*** - *"The LORD is on my side; I will not fear: what can man do unto me?"*
- ***Matthew 10:28*** - *"Do not be afraid of those who kill the body but cannot kill the soul. Rather, be afraid of the One who can destroy both soul and body in hell."*
- ***Psalms 34:19*** - *"Many are the afflictions of the righteous: but the LORD delivereth him out of them all."*
- ***Romans 8:18*** - *"For I reckon that the sufferings of this present time are not worthy to be compared with the glory which shall be revealed in us."*
- ***Isaiah 50:6-10*** -*" ⁶I gave my back to the smiters, and my cheeks to them that plucked off the hair: I hid not my face from shame and spitting. ⁷For the Lord GOD will help me; therefore, shall I not be confounded: therefore, have I set my face like a flint, and I know that I shall not be ashamed. ⁸He is near that justifieth me; who will contend with me? let us stand together: who is mine adversary? let him come near to me. ⁹Behold, the Lord GOD will help me; who is he that shall condemn me? lo, they all shall wax old as a garment; the moth shall eat them up."*
- ***Psalms 27:1-10*** *"The LORD is my light and my salvation; whom shall I fear? the LORD is the strength of my life; of whom shall I be afraid? ²When the wicked, even mine enemies and my foes, came upon me to eat up my flesh, they stumbled and fell. ³Though a host should encamp against me, my heart shall not fear: though war should rise against me, in this will I be confident. ⁴One thing have I desired of the LORD, that will I seek after; that I may dwell in the house of the LORD all the days of my life, to behold the beauty of the LORD, and to enquire in his temple. ⁵For in the time of trouble he shall hide me in his pavilion: in the secret of his tabernacle shall he hide me; he shall set me up upon a rock. ⁶And now shall mine head*

How To Avoid Quitting

be lifted up above mine enemies round about me: therefore, will I offer in his tabernacle sacrifices of joy; I will sing, yea, I will sing praises unto the LORD. ⁷Hear, O LORD, when I cry with my voice: have mercy also upon me, and answer me. ⁸When thou saidst, Seek ye my face; my heart said unto thee, Thy face, LORD, will I seek. ⁹Hide not thy face far from me; put not thy servant away in anger: thou hast been my help; leave me not, neither forsake me, O God of my salvation. ¹⁰When my father and my mother forsake me, then the LORD will take me up."

As often as I could, I read and confessed these scriptures at least two (2) times a day! Eventually, my reading went from reading to REVELATION, from a confession to a CONVICTION!

It was after reading **Psalms 118:6** that a light really came on in my spirit and I realized with a strong conviction that GOD was with me!

Psalms 118:6 – *"The LORD is on my side; I will not fear: what can man do unto me?"* It was what some folks call an "AH... HA..." moment! My spiritual eye opened up and the Baptist ministerial training kicked in, to the point that I started breaking this passage down in the following manner:

<u>*"The LORD is on my side:"*</u> The LORD- KING of ALL KINGS, the LORD OF ALL LORDS, and the creator of ALL things. The one who raised the dead and healed the sick. The one who hung, bled and died, but rose with ALL POWER!

<u>*"is on my side:"*</u> On "MY" side! I started making it personal. On "MY" (Earl Dixon) side! He's right there with me (Earl Dixon)! He has my (Earl Dixon) back!

The light really came on! GOD IS WITH ME (EARL DIXON)! Upon this revelation my conversations about my situation changed too. When I tell you a peace came over my life like I had NEVER felt before! You too need to understand that whether guilty or not, if you've accepted Jesus as your personal Lord and Savior of your life, HE'S WITH YOU *(Insert your name here reader)* TOO!

I love the many revelations that the psalmist had concerning God's presence in his life! Naturally, many immediately think of the 23rd Psalm as reassurance of his presence in our lives during troubled times. But Psalm 27 ended up becoming my favorite to lean upon in times of need!

I won't elaborate on it. But I encourage you to read it and allow the words in bold print to minister to you:

Psalm 27

"¹The LORD is my light and my salvation—
so why should I be afraid?
The LORD is my fortress, protecting me from danger,
so why should I tremble?
²When evil people come to devour me,
when my enemies and foes attack me,
they will stumble and fall.
³Though a mighty army surrounds me,
my heart will not be afraid.
Even if I am attacked,
I will remain confident.
⁴The one thing I ask of the LORD—
the thing I seek most—
is to live in the house of the LORD all the days of my life,

How To Avoid Quitting

*delighting in the LORD's perfections
and meditating in his Temple.*
**⁵ For he will conceal me there when troubles come;
he will hide me in his sanctuary.
He will place me out of reach on a high rock.
⁶ Then I will hold my head high
above my enemies who surround me.**
*At his sanctuary I will offer sacrifices with shouts of joy,
singing and praising the LORD with music.
⁷ Hear me as I pray, O LORD.
Be merciful and answer me!
⁸ My heart has heard you say, "Come and talk with me."
And my heart responds, "LORD, I am coming."
⁹ Do not turn your back on me.
Do not reject your servant in anger.*
You have always been my helper.
*Don't leave me now; don't abandon me,
O God of my salvation!
¹⁰ Even if my father and mother abandon me,*
the LORD will hold me close."

I challenge you to pray and ask God for a revelation of the words that I have in bold print, to be engraved in your spirit. KNOWING that God is present with you at all times will empower you with so much strength, courage, and faith until it will amaze you!

CHAPTER 3

STAND ON GOD'S WORD

Psalm 119:46-52 *"Remember the word to Your servant, Upon which You have caused me to hope.* ⁵⁰ *This is my comfort in my affliction, For Your word has given me life.* ⁵¹ *The proud have me in great derision, Yet I do not turn aside from Your law.* ⁵² *I remembered Your judgments of old, O* LORD, *And have comforted myself."*

In her album, Bringing It All Together, Vickie Winans sang, "We need a word from the Lord. Just one word from the Lord to soothe all doubt." I discovered in real life that it's true! One word from God can and will change the whole trajectory of your life. If you are not a student of the Bible I make no apologies. I assure you as a preacher of the gospel for over thirty (30) years, I'm convinced that there is nothing any of us can encounter, which has not been solved in the HOLY BIBLE!

Although many believers have not given much evidence to this, there is a power in the word of God that will give you the strength to conquer and overcome anything!

I remember sitting in on a meeting with some local pastors and their bishop. I was there by invitation only. This meant that my role was to sit, be quiet, and observe the order of the meeting. This was a time in my life when I was hurting internally, feeling rejected by the masses and God; wondering to myself how He could allow me to experience this awful situation!

While masking all of this internal hurt and shame, all of a sudden the Bishop introduced a man who appeared to be from another country. This man begins to encourage each pastor present with a word in which I will NEVER forget. He spoke of the stresses and challenges in ministry and what we should do in times of adversities. He encouraged us to REMIND GOD of the words that He/God had spoken to us. Then as he begins to quote **Psalm 119:46-52** it was as if these words came alive to ONLY ME! As I listened, I felt a quickening in my spirit which spoke loud and clear to my inner man! Those words were, *"God I admit I hate with a passion where I am and what I'm feeling right now. Yes, it hurts, it's shameful and downright unfair! But beyond all of this, I KNOW there are words and promises that you've spoken to me from your word in my own personal time with you! Jesus REMEMBER the good things, the successes and the pleasures you've spoken to me!"* Upon hearing this man quote **Psalms 119:46-52**, my situation didn't change immediately. Nevertheless, there was an IMMEDIATE REFRESHING which came over me that to this day, is difficult to describe to its fullest!

One thing I know and am sure of today, **THE WORD OF GOD WAS MY WAY OUT!** What I later discovered, even as a Pastor, was culturally I had been MEMORIZING and ENJOYING the Word, as opposed to taking it in and ALLOWING IT TO COME ALIVE IN ME!

How To Avoid Quitting

I was eager to get home and study in great depth the words of Psalms 119:46-52. It was EVERYTHING I FELT and DESIRED to say to God. It was then that I understood God hastens to perform HIS Word and NOT OURS! Yes, our Daddy hears the faith and the cries of His children. But I learned He's more apt to respond and bring HIS word to pass, not mine.

Let's take a closer look at Psalm 119:46-52:

- ***"Remember the word to your servant..."*** In our most trying times, we must REMIND GOD of His Word! The words that you know God spoke to you at the start of an assignment and throughout the course of you carrying it out! Understanding also that God already knows what He said, but recognizing that it's really about you being able to vocalize again from your own mouth. In addition to you knowing that death and life is in the power of our tongues. Doing this also forces you to move pass the painful emotions that you feel. It forces you to speak with power and authority, all that you knew before any of those things happened.

A good friend of mine simply says, **"In your day of CONTRADICTION, DON'T CHANGE YOUR FAITH CONFESSION!"** While this moment may be a surprise to you, it isn't a surprise to God. God knew when He spoke to you every good, bad or indifferent circumstance/situation that was destined to take place in your life. If it didn't stop Him from speaking it into your life, IT SHOULDN'T STOP YOU FROM CONFESSING IT TO MANIFEST IN YOUR LIFE NOW!

- ***"Upon which You have caused me to hope..."*** I learned that my HOPE must ALWAYS come from a God whose words will NEVER return void! As I was being reminded of the things I knew in my heart God had spoken over my life; my hope was diminished. What God had spoken was not what I was experiencing! Pain tried to overcome me, so I practiced THINKING MORE on what I knew God said in an effort to combat the negative feelings and thoughts. Thoughts like, *"you are done… it's over… God is never going to use you as He did in previous years!"*

NOTE: I said I had to PRACTICE! I use this term because in my spirit I knew and believed ALL that God had spoken to me, but simultaneously EVERYDAY I felt the pain of my negative state of affairs. That was my REALITY! I have to be honest. Just like exercising… sometimes I won, sometimes I didn't! But like everything else, if you are consistent with your practice long enough, you will gain the edge and build strong mental muscles to combat the enemy!

- *"50 This is my comfort in my affliction, For Your word has given me life…"* The one thing that blesses me with this statement is the psalmist serves as evidence to me. Evidence that FAITH isn't denying my realities, but simply acknowledging its reality and being steadfast in KNOWING God will bring me through! The psalmist made me comfortable in acknowledging my hurt and pain, but at the same time he revealed WHERE I and HOW I could LIVE, even in this horrible situation!

Since then, my word to anyone who may be experiencing a horrible situation or might be in the FAITH FIGHT of their life, is to BURY YOUR MIND in the Word of God!

- *"51 The proud have me in great derision, Yet I do not turn aside from Your law. 52 I remembered Your judgments of old, O Lord, And have comforted myself..."* My rationale was, if the psalmist could make such a bold statement, then certainly I could too! The psalmist says, *"in the midst of this derision,* (which is: CONTEMPTUOUS ridicule or mockery) *he would not stray from God's word!"* As I stated in a previous chapter, God's Word was my comfort! As a pastor whom God has privileged to oversee and serve hundreds of people, one thing I dislike is when seasoned believers encounter the hardships of life. In these moments, RARELY do we find believers who look to the Word of God for the answer! Often in many cases, we respond no different than people who have no revelation of God! There is a slogan of a local church in our city which says, **"The Word of God is the Answer!"** For years I preached and taught this! Most importantly, in the greatest time of affliction, I found this to be true!

NOTE: WHATEVER situation you are in, search with diligence God's Word for stories, words or passages of scripture which are relevant to your situation and/or circumstance. Read them as often as you can. Don't just read or memorize them, but as you read, allow the Holy Spirit to speak to you concerning those passages. Then decree and declare them out loud! You will see those words come alive in your life and provide comfort until the storm is over!

Earl Dixon

Chapter 4

GET IN FAITH

I hate to tell you, but if you are consistently contemplating quitting, **YOU ARE NOT IN FAITH!** No person truly living a LIFESTYLE of faith is in a constant state of worry or operating with a quitter's mentality. Faith always believes! Unfortunately, many people in the church are not living faith filled lives. Having a life filled with diverse faith acts is not the same as living in faith.

Right in the midst of my fears and disappointments, I met a young man who had been a viewer of a local TV broadcast that I once had. This was before all my troubles began. I was getting a shave in a barbershop that he owned. He proceeded to talk about how much I inspired him and how he would stay up late waiting for us to come on the air. Well, as fate would have it, we bonded and became really good friends in a span of one year.

This is one of the most positive people I had ever known. He was always speaking faith and NEVER had room for doubt of any kind. He was so positive that his positivity became annoying at times.

Earl Dixon

It was September 6 (my birthday) and my friend decided to treat me to a very nice dinner at a local restaurant. We ate and talked about one faith subject after another. I then noticed he became very serious. He said, "Pastor, at this point you know I respect you as a person and a man of God? I need to share something with you."

Well in my head I'm thinking… it's my birthday. He must be about to tell me something big that God had told him to bless me with. Quite the contrary! He looks at me and says, "Pastor, you are not in faith!" As he proceeded to tell me, in my mind I'm thinking how over twenty (20) years ago, with a wife and small child, I left a decent paying job in a local plant because I believed God called me into full-time ministry. One time I took $12,000.00 at one time and sowed $1000.00 each to twelve (12) different churches and through God's help, we took a small church on the back side of nowhere and God did tremendous things with a small group of people. As he talked, I thought about without being fought or forced out, I resigned from a ministry of fourteen (14) years full of people that I loved. Many of these people were very kind to my family and I. I left all of that because I believed God said my time was over and there was another assignment for me to complete. Still, you tell me I'm not in faith? I knew in my heart that this man loved me and was definitely on my side. Therefore, wisdom said at least listen to the brother.

Without appearing to be upset or offended, I heard him out. It was after that dinner on the way home, God spoke to me and it left me amazed! He said and I quote: *"Earl, you are like most believers who think they're in faith! You have no fear of moving or performing faith acts as long as you believe I (God) told you. The problem is when you have to **STAND** for long periods of time in faith,*

How To Avoid Quitting

that's when you get out of faith and often times seek to help me (GOD) do what I promised. Earl, a LIFESTYLE of Faith is a life that's TOTALLY confident and convinced without fear of contradiction, that I will do everything I said!

As I wept and accepted every word, I knew what God had spoken was true. I then begin to repent for the times knowingly and unknowingly that I didn't trust Him. I repented for how I hurt situations by getting in the way and seeking to fix only what He alone could do. It was at this very moment that I had to start the journey of LIVING BY FAITH and not a life FULL OF FAITH ACTS! But how Lord…how?

For me it started with a commitment to trust and believe God's Word. Regardless of the circumstances, I had to learn what I call the mechanics of faith. I revisited and examined the Bible's meaning of what faith is and fed my spirit man with as much faith teaching as possible.

Perhaps you too haven't really been in faith. I urge you to be sure and practice on a daily basis, living a faith filled life.

According to God's word to me, a faith filled life or a LIFESTYLE of FAITH is: ***a life that is convinced and sure that whatever God promised, He's able to perform. It's a life of confidence, one that is free of the stress and worry of life and its circumstances.***

In the words of Dr. Mike Murdock, "MY PRECIOUS FRIEND… anything that is not of FAITH is SIN!" If you are experiencing sleepless nights, days of worrying, and consistent desires to quit, I'm sorry…YOU ARE NOT IN FAITH!

Faith breathes confidence, assurance; as well as a strong attitude that believes GOD period!

So how does one get into faith? Romans 10:17 says (KJV), *"⁴⁷ So then faith cometh by hearing, and hearing by the word of God."* Faith, like everything else, must be practiced. I believe that for one to have an effective and bountiful faith life, faith must be completed in steps and/or phases. Faith is action. With that being said, there is nothing wrong with you taking small steps and increasing them as time progresses. Today, through the internet and social media we have an assortment of things to hear and see. You turn on social media and people everywhere have something to say about everything. But, the key to getting back into faith is HEARING the Gospel of the Kingdom of GOD.

Contrary to what many will tell you, it is imperative that you make adequate time to hear and be involved with the Word of God! Nonetheless, it's one thing to hear and another to believe. Believing is so important because Romans 10:10-17 states, *"with the heart man BELIEVES…"*

For example, maybe you are attempting to rebound from a traumatic situation which has caused you to not trust people. My suggestion would be for you to try to open up to at least one person, while keeping in mind, that people are human. Consciously, you should know that you can't allow a perceived negative response from another person to cause you to shut down and build up a wall again.

Perhaps you are overcoming a very painful divorce. Before you try dating again, you must accept the fact that all people aren't the same. Therefore, don't make the mistake of holding a new love interest to an unrealistic expectation, resulting from the pain of the last relationship you were in.

How To Avoid Quitting

Getting back in faith has become a simple four (4) step process for me. If followed correctly, you willl be back in faith in no time as well!

1. **Hearing**
2. **Believing**
3. **Confessing**
4. **Corresponding Actions**

As a pastor, I always found it somewhat interesting to see thousands upon thousands in the church to hear, while simultaneously it's so difficult to get people to believe. Believing is important for several biblical reasons.

Romans 10:14 ESV states. "How then will they call on him in whom they have not believed? And how are they to believe in him of whom they have never heard? And how are they to hear without someone preaching?"

Hebrews 11:6 says, *"But without faith it is impossible to please him: for he that cometh to God must believe that he is, and that he is a rewarder of them that diligently seek him."*

How can one say that they are praying, but in their heart, praying to a God they don't trust or believe in? Your believing is crucial to pleasing God. God is not pleased when His children don't have the faith to believe that He can bring a healing and calm to their situations.

After believing, you must move into the confessing phase of faith. I've learned that when one really believes something, others will know it because you will speak it.

Mark 11:23 *"Truly, I say to you, whoever says to this mountain, 'Be taken up and thrown into the sea,' and does not doubt in his heart, but believes that what he says will come to pass, it will be done for him."*

Undeniably when you hear, believe, and confess by faith, you will have corresponding actions that will line up with your belief and confession.

Romans 4:19-21 *[19] And being not weak in faith, he considered not his own body now dead, when he was about an hundred years old, neither yet the deadness of Sarah's womb: [20] He staggered not at the promise of God through unbelief; but was strong in faith, giving glory to God; [21] And being fully persuaded that, what he had promised, he was able also to perform.*

My pastor always said, *"Don't tell me you are praying for a job and haven't put in one application. Don't say you are believing God for a home and you are not taking the steps involved with purchasing a home!"* Getting in faith is so vital because you won't get God's supernatural help in doubt or disbelief. Therefore, corresponding actions will move and push you right into the direction of what you are believing God to do!

What I found out the hard way was this: all four must be in effect. Hearing, believing and confessing without corresponding actions won't work.

You must practice operating all four!

Maybe you are reading and you are willing to admit like I did that you have no problems acting in faith. But, you too have the most challenges when having to stand or wait in faith.

Don't beat yourself up, simply repent and ask God to give you another chance, and begin your daily journey of LIVING by FAITH for real!

Chapter 5

LET GO OF BITTERNESS!

I've NEVER broadcasted that I was a perfect man. Yet, anyone who really knows me recognizes that one of my greatest attributes is giving. I am a giver and although I pride myself on this truth, there were valuable lessons that I had to learn concerning giving. These lessons literally freed me from the bitterness I was experiencing.

Years ago God was really blessing me through the wonderful generosity of people whom I pastored. I recall preaching for many churches without receiving honorariums. Why? Because my heart was never to go to a church and take, but to give. Often times, if I sensed that a ministry was going through some type of struggle, I would tell the ministry to give what they intended for me directly to the Pastor or to the event in which they were hosting.

There were several others who knew I was doing pretty good who would call upon me to assist with their financial challenges, and without hesitation I'd respond. There are many situations where we blessed people just for the sake of blessing. I was such a giver that my family would often tell me that they wouldn't give me anything material because I would eventually give it away.

The problem when I assumed that people would treat you like you treated them. This is where all the bitterness came from. It wasn't just the fact that my character and integrity was being condemned, I just expected that someone would look beyond what was being said and see the man who ALWAYS did whatever he could to help others.

I anticipated that someone would throw us a lifeline! My family was struggling terribly. From our point of view, it looked as if many of the ones who could help, enjoyed watching us fail. I supposed upon hearing what was happening to me and my family, that many of the same people we helped over the years would provide some type of assistance to us. Well… that didn't happen! As a result, I became very angry and bitter because I knew many people who could have helped us and unfortunately they didn't.

Still, God always has an unexpected ram in the bush. God sent a man who my family and I will NEVER forget. I only call his name out of respect and gratitude, Bishop Theo Bailey Jr.! There were people who were kind to us here and there, but Bishop Bailey threw us the LIFELINE that we needed!

I remember times when he would call and for hours, Bishop Bailey Jr. would speak life into us. I recall this one occasion when my wife was working at a local bank where we also banked too. This man just came one day and voluntarily put $2000.00 in our account. Then there were other times when he would call and his direct words would be, *"Pastor Dixon, don't give me the faith answer, but how are you doing? Are your bills paid?"* I can go on and on with the things Bishop Theo Bailey Jr. did, while speaking life into us too.

How To Avoid Quitting

One day while in an angry and bitter state of mind, I shared with him how livid I was with family, ministers, and people in general, who did very little to come to our aide. It was then that Bishop Bailey Jr. said to me these words in which I will never forget. He said, *"Earl… you may as well release those people so God can bless you. The bible doesn't say you reap* **WHERE** *you sow. But you reap* **WHAT** *you sow!"* He said, *"Son… you are looking to the wrong people for your harvest!* **God owes you, not the people you helped!"**

At that very moment liberation came over me! Even though I had read Galatian 6:7, *"Be not deceived; God is not mocked: for whatsoever a man soweth,* **THAT** *shall he also reap."* I never saw it in the way that I did that day.

Bishop Bailey Jr. also said, *"Earl… you are a good man and you've certainly help many people. But from now on… anything you do for anyone, make sure you are doing it unto the Lord. For His returns far outweigh any man's."* I allowed the influence of that revelation to simmer in my spirit and the bitterness I had begun to leave.

Once I got through that stage, I remember another situation that helped me. I discovered that it was also possible that many people weren't ignoring our situation. They just may not have been aware of what was really going on in our lives.

It was the statement of another pastor that made me realize that **we should NEVER assume people know things that we ourselves haven't specifically told them.**

I told him how I once was bitter with him but no longer was. His reply was liberating as well. He said, *"Earl… I didn't know the magnitude of what was going on because every time I saw you or your family, you guys always walked in an image that said you all were doing well."*

I boast in this now because I never want to walk in a manner that reveals hurt, struggle or pain. One thing we were taught was, you don't have to look like where you are. Yes, we struggled, but my wife and I have always prided ourselves on the fact that we would not project a poor, struggling, and needy image! Therefore, in that regard, we were people who walked with our heads up, not trying to drop pity lines to get people to respond to our needs.

I challenge you to consider what image you are portraying. Could you be bitter with people who really have no clue of the real pain you are suffering? Even if you feel your situation is opposite of ours, being a carrier of the spirit of bitterness is NEVER good for anyone!

Bitterness is resentful cynicism that results in an intense antagonism or hostility towards others. The Bible teaches us in Ephesians 4:31 to *"get rid of all bitterness, rage and anger, brawling and slander, along with every form of malice."* The scripture goes on to tell us how to deal with such bitterness and its fruits, by being *"kind and compassionate to one another, forgiving each other, just as in Christ God forgave you."* The scriptures reads as follows:

- **<u>Ephesians 4:31-32</u>** *¹Let all bitterness, and wrath, and anger, and clamour, and evil speaking, be put away from you, with all malice: ³²And be ye kind one to another, tenderhearted, forgiving one another, even as God for Christ's sake hath forgiven you.*

The word *bitter* means *"sharp like an arrow or pungent to the taste, disagreeable; venomous."* The idea is that of the poisonous water given to the women who were suspected of committing adultery in Numbers 5:18: *"the bitter water that brings a curse."* In its figurative sense *bitterness* refers to a mental or emotional state that corrodes or "eats_away at." Bitterness is that state of mind which willfully holds on to angry feelings, ready to take offense, and able to break out in anger at any moment. **The forth most danger in succumbing to bitterness and allowing it to rule our hearts is: it is a spirit that refuses reconciliation.** As a result, bitterness leads to wrath, which is the explosion on the outside of the feelings on the inside. Such unbridled wrath and anger often lead to "brawling" which is the brash self-absorption of an angry person who needs to make everyone hear his grievances. Another evil brought on by bitterness is slander. All this then leads to a spirit of malice, which signifies evil-mindedness or feelings of intense hatred. This kind of attitude is sensual and devilish in its influences. Malice is a deliberate attempt to harm another person. Therefore, "every form of malice" must be done away with (Ephesians 4:31). We must always be wary of allowing "bitter roots" to grow in our hearts. Such roots will cause us to fall short of the grace of God. God's will is that His people live in love, joy, peace, and holiness; not in bitterness. Therefore, the believer must always watch diligently, being on guard against the grave peril of bitterness *(cited from https://www.gotquestions.org/Bible-bitterness.html).*

Chapter 6
KILL ENTITLEMENT

Another hard but great lesson I learned on this journey was **NO ONE OWED ME ANYTHING!**

Without question there were so many admirable things that I had done for many people; family, friends, ministers, local churches, business people, and a host of strangers. It was the statement that Bishop Bailey Jr. made one day that caused me to do several things. I was ultimately led me to kill what I call a *Spirit of Entitlement!* Bishop Bailey Jr. spoke these simple words which immediately brought liberation to my spirit. He said **"Earl... you better get over that quick because the bible said you reap WHAT you sow, not WHERE you sowed."**

This was such a liberating revelation. With everything I was facing, my thoughts were simply this, *"If all the people that I've helped over the years would do something for me, then at least my financial troubles would go away!"* After all, at that time I felt like and knew I had helped so many! However, the more optimistic I was that many would hear of what was happening and lend their aide and support, the more time passed.

Maybe your situational need is not financial such as mine? It could be that you are looking to bounce back from something totally different. Whatever the situation may be, please be thankful to anyone in your family or inner circle, who does help! I had to accept the hard truth, and that was; **NO ONE OWED ME ANYTHING!**

With God's help, take responsibility for your own recovery and watch God begin to do wonders in your plan for restoration.

Now, I know I shared this with you previously. But, you must understand and wrap your brain around the impact of this statement. While aware of all of the people that I helped and did well for, I got happy! I got happy because if there was one thing that I did know, I knew I had sowed much seed of good deeds into the lives of many!

Entitlement is simply you feeling like you have the right to something. It's you feeling overwhelmingly deserving of something. Again, in your case other people may owe you favors. Still, you cannot sit around and look for other people to be responsible for you rebounding from your setback. You probably feel as I once did! *"Why yes! They should help me… They should volunteer and offer support."* In some cases, that may be true. Still, you can't sit around waiting for a favor, a handout, or support from people. Take responsibility for your own comeback. Get diligent in doing so, and God will touch the right people in whom He has commanded to bless you.

The Prophet Elijah in **I Kings 17:8-16**, was instructed by God to go to Zarephath. It was in there that God commanded a widow woman to provide what the prophet needed for sustainment during this time of famine. What we

How To Avoid Quitting

don't see is a man looking for a handout or waiting for some person to help him. We see a man hearing and responding to the instructions of God. Although Elijah was in a famine, he had several things going for him;

1. God was with him.
2. He was familiar with God's voice.
3. He was obedient to God's instruction.

As you go forth, keep a posture to hear, know, and move on God's instruction; while being confident in knowing that your famine will be over in no time.

Right now, release anyone that you feel should be there for you in your time of need. Kill that spirit of entitlement and move forward in your restoration plan!

Get up and know that GOD owes you, not man! Believe me when I tell you, NO ONE pays the way God does. Release every person who didn't come through for you. Release every family member or friend who you feel gloated during your struggle or fall. God is not going to release what's yours, until you release the hurt and bitterness of entitlement!

Entitlement is reflected almost everywhere in the world today! Take an athlete who already has made more millions than he or she could spend in a lifetime. Yet, many will request the restructuring of their contract because they feel they are entitled to more! In most cases, if they don't get what's requested, the end result is sitting out during training camp or an entire season.

It is also said that millennials are a generation of young people who were born with a sense of entitlement. Many researchers of the millennial generation refer to this group as spoiled and entitled. Whether the research is true or false, I believe entitlement is something that we all have had to deal with at one time or another. The problem with this is, when you develop entitlement it can also bring unrealistic expectations of other people simply on the basis of you feeling owed.

When it comes to you overcoming whatever it is that has you shutting down on life, contemplating suicide, or checking out because of a setback, you must rise above your entitlement mentality.

Again, no one owes you anything! The mentality of entitlement can only yield the result of unnecessary mental, physical, and spiritual pain. Particularly when you have expectations of others and not God! Remember the words which liberated me, *"YOU REAP WHAT YOU SOW… NOT WHERE YOU SOWED!"*

CHAPTER 7

AVOID MAKING DESPERATE MOVES

The same things that caused of lot of my problems, were some of the same things that prolonged the pain.

Mark 5:24-34 "24 *So Jesus went with him a large crowd followed and pressed around him.* 25 *And a woman was there who had been subject to bleeding for twelve years.* 26 *She had suffered a great deal under the care of many doctors and had spent all she had, yet instead of getting better she grew worse.* 27 *When she heard about Jesus, she came up behind him in the crowd and touched his cloak,* 28 *because she thought, "If I just touch his clothes, I will be healed."* 29 *Immediately her bleeding stopped and she felt in her body that she was freed from her suffering.* 30 *At once Jesus realized that power had gone out from him. He turned around in the crowd and asked, "Who touched my clothes?"* 31 *"You see the people crowding against you," his disciples answered, "and yet you can ask, 'Who touched me?'"* 32 *But Jesus kept looking around to see who had done it.* 33 *Then the woman, knowing what had happened to her, came and fell at his feet and, trembling with fear, told him the whole truth.* 34 *He said to her, "Daughter, your faith has healed you. Go in peace and be freed from your suffering."*

There are two sides of desperation. In my opinion, the woman with the issue of blood is a good picture of a desperate person trying to get relief from a twelve (12) year issue. While we give her credit for her persistence and her willingness to not stop until she got healed, I would like to hypothetically pose a question: **What if she had gone to Jesus from the start?**

Can you imagine what her life would have been like if she would have gone to Jesus from the start? I would venture to believe that she would have saved money and time at the doctor, and her suffering would not have lasted as long as it did. Here's the point I'm trying to make, I honestly believe in times of desperation we must be very careful not to be sidetracked by quick fixes and other means that are absent of plans that are orchestrated by God. Being desperate to get out before time will also open you up to the vulnerability of unnecessary time and monetary loss. You see, before I got to the place of being able to embrace the pain and isolation, I did everything I thought possible to come out. Many times I did not wait on God's help. Therefore, believe me when I tell you, I wasted so much money and time trying stuff that I never should have tried. When I think on it today, I hurt over the money I could have used to pay people instead of trying a lot of the quick fixes that never work for me either. This doesn't mean those things were bad, they just weren't for me! They were things I should not have tried!

I'm what I call a "go-getter." A "go-getter" is a person that knows how to make things happen and get them done. The only problem with that is, **the same things that caused of lot of my problems, were some of the same things that prolonged the pain.**

How To Avoid Quitting

There were several areas where I lacked discipline. As a result, many times I tried to use the quick fixes of multilevel marketing businesses to come out of the financial hardships that I was facing. From selling insurance, diet pills, and all kinds of get rich quick ideas, I only got into deeper trouble financially. Even in my giving, I KNOW and BELIEVE you NEVER go wrong in giving. But today, I'm very careful not to be moved by preachers who say GOD said give certain seeds and God is going do this or that for you.

I remember years ago, I had just received a $5000.00 plus tax refund check. I heard a minister, whom I still highly respect, was in town. He said for every person who sowed $1000.00, he would pray and ask God every time he would get blessed, that God would bless us as well. He called it a BOAZ anointing. I knew that man was very wealthy in the natural and I respected him, so it sounded like a good deal to me. Besides, I'm a giver to the core and had the $1000.00, so the request wasn't much of a stretch for me! I gave the $1000 and all I know is after that, I literally lost everything I had; all but my wife and kids! **PLEASE don't take this the wrong way because I believe this man to be <u>a true man of God</u>.** I also listen to him today.

What I discovered was this, it had nothing to do with him; I sowed, but not in FAITH! I sowed in desperation! I know it wasn't faith because after all, I had that and a few thousands more! This is why I believe many believers who sow thousands are frustrated, they are sowing and giving, **but not in FAITH!**

Please don't use this as a means to validate being stingy, or for the reason why you don't give in church; and don't you dare stop listening to men of God because of this one instance in my life! Although what he said hasn't happened, I believe that seed eventually produced some fruit in my life.

Again, the Holy Spirit revealed to me it wasn't the man of God's appeal, it was me! I sowed a seed out of a desperate heart to get free and not in faith and in that particular case, it didn't work! Trust me when I tell you, there have been many other times where I sowed in faith and God moved!

One instance was the time when I sowed $550.00 at my pastor's appreciation and walked away (that same day) with $5,000.00. All I'm saying is, **when you are in a very tight and painful financial place, it's imperative that you don't give out of your emotions.** Truth is, I should have made paying my debt the priority. Again, I want to say this carefully because there are times when I believe God will honor your seed in an expeditious manner with a supernatural blessing. **Nevertheless, be careful to make sure you are led of your spirit and not by your pain.**

Today, get rich quick businesses are becoming increasingly popular almost everywhere. Desperate to come out of their financially strapped situations, many people are spending millions of dollars trying to come back monetarily. The only problem with this scenario is if you lack discipline and/or diligence, you will find yourself spending money on materials which could have been used to pay bills.

What if your problem isn't mostly financial like mine? Maybe you've been hurt by a life event of some type. My answer is this, don't be like the woman in Mark 5:24-36, spending all of your energy on self-efforts that God didn't instruct. Spend your efforts seeking God. I know believers today haven't been great in demonstrating that God and the church are the solution to your problems. **However, I'm thoroughly** convinced that they are! With God **ALL** things are possible! Despite the negative press and commentary the church receives today, I still believe there's help in the house and word of God!

There is a local pastor in our city whom I highly respect. Often I've heard him say, *"Did God tell you to do that? I don't care how good something sounds as well as how much someone else might be profiting from it, at the end of the day, make sure God is instructing YOU!"*

If you are going to be desperate, use your desperation to go after God. Today, I can honestly say it was my pursuit of God that brought me out. It was hours in His Word, listening to hours of good preaching, hours in prayer that developed the greatest asset I've ever known! ***An EAR to HEAR and DISCERN the VOICE of GOD!***

I learned the hard way to do what the woman with the issue of blood did. Do whatever I needed to do; go through whatever I needed to go through to get in the presence of Jesus! Like this woman, there are many obstacles when you are in a hard place that will seek to stop you. But you must PUSH through them!

Many times I didn't FEEL like studying, praying, giving my tithe, and even going to church, BUT I DID! Over the years I've had many ministers come to me for advice. One of the main things I share with them is this, **"The greatest asset that we all have as believers is our ability to HEAR and DISCERN GOD'S VOICE."**

Whether it's through a preacher, the bible, in prayer or whatever means God chooses to use in our lives, being in a place to hear and be touched by God is the key to <u>not</u> making a desperate move!

What if you are having problems hearing, discerning or understanding the voice of God? Then seek wise counsel! Here are four (4) very fascinating scripture verses telling us that there is safety in the multitude of counselors. Without appropriate counsel with others our plans can go awry, and we are to wage war by having wise counsel with others.

> *"A wise man is strong, yes, a man of knowledge increases strength; for by wise counsel you will wage your own war, and in a multitude of counselors there is safety."* (Proverbs 24:5)

> *"Without counsel, plans go awry, but in the multitude of counselors they are established."* (Proverbs 15:22)

> *"Every purpose is established by counsel; by wise counsel wage war."* (Proverbs 20:18)

> *"Where there is no counsel, the people fall; but in the multitude of counselors there is safety."* (Proverbs 11:14)

How To Avoid Quitting

The Bible tells us that all men will only "know in part". As a result, no one person will ever have all of the answers to everything in this life. By having a group of solid Christian friends you can hash things out with, you will help keep each other up and sharp in the Lord and in your life.

Earl Dixon

CHAPTER 8

GET A NEW STRATEGY

Luke 5:4-9 *"4 Now when he had left speaking, he said unto Simon, Launch out into the deep, and let down your nets for a draught. 5 And Simon answering said unto him, Master, we have toiled all the night, and have taken nothing: nevertheless at thy word I will let down the net. 6 And when they had this done, they enclosed a great multitude of fishes: and their net brake. 7 And they beckoned unto their partners, which were in the other ship, that they should come and help them. And they came, and filled both the ships, so that they began to sink. 8 When Simon Peter saw it, he fell down at Jesus' knees, saying, Depart from me; for I am a sinful man, O Lord. 9 For he was astonished, and all that were with him, at the draught of the fishes which they had taken."*

Another refreshing experience was the discovery of needing a NEW STRATEGY. I get upset when I think about all the time I wasted being surprised by the betrayals, embarrassed by my so-called failures, and disappointed in my decisions. Many of which prolonged my comeback and restoration!

As I wasted day after day sobbing, time was still moving. I remember practically falling into a depressed state because I felt like at this stage in my life, I should be much further along and in a much better place!

One morning while lying in bed, my thoughts almost got the best of me. I was preparing to celebrate twenty-five (25) years of ministry, twenty-five (25) years of marriage, and fifty (50) years of life. As I laid in bed I thought to myself, I'm almost fifty (50) years old, I live upstairs above my church, I've suffered one loss after another, experienced lots of damaged relationships, and have lost nearly everything except my wife and children. Even they, at times, said things which sounded like they were here because they literally had nothing and nowhere else to go! I was so crushed. Everything that I hated as a child and vowed would NEVER happen to me, seemed to have slapped me in the face day after day!

But GOD! I heard a preacher say in a message that God was going to do something NEW and FRESH all in the same place that you once failed. He preached from John 5 where Peter and the others had been out all night and caught nothing. God specifically spoke several things to me in this message and I share them with you below:

1. He/God settled the fact that I didn't have to leave town and start over, as I so often contemplated.
2. He/God can turn my present failures into triumphs; in the same place that I failed.
3. ALL I NEEDED was a NEW strategy!

People have committed suicide due to the mere fact that things which they disparately desired didn't happen. Many lose their minds and check out mentally because they felt life dealt them a hand they will never be able to overcome. Not

How To Avoid Quitting

me! I knew I could win over what was lost, thank God for what was left, and move on to bigger or greater things.

I'm an adamant college football fan. One my favorite coaches is Nick Saban of the Alabama Crimson Tide (also my favorite college team). He's one of my favorites because he doesn't mind changing strategies midstream. His teams have always been known for having strong offensive and defensive lines. From an offensive standpoint, Alabama was known for overpowering defenses with these lines. Also, with QB's who didn't have to be great, only good at managing these offenses that literally overpowered you with their running game. Currently, the game has changed to a point where most teams are now running what they call pro style spread offenses. Therefore, Nick has had to change his strategy and the results are amazing!

Many nights I contemplated, should I change my strategy and set new goals, visions, and instruction? Or, should I keep whining over what happened? I chose the former. I realized there is nothing wrong with changing strategies. After all, God did too.

When you understand the KINGDOM order of God, you see that it was NEVER in the plan of God for man to operate as we are on the earth today. If you go back to creation, you will discover God's original intent was for man to live in His kingdom, ruling, and having dominion on the earth with God as our SOLE source of supply. But since the fall of Adam, God is using his Word, prophets, pastors, teachers, apostles and evangelists (Ephesians 4:11) to bring man back to his original place in the garden.

If you are ever going to come back and be restored from your place of failure, you must pray for another strategy! God gives great strategies and instruction. He instructed Peter and the others to launch out from the same boat, in the same water, using the same nets, but this time on the RIGHT SIDE. I don't know what your RIGHT SIDE may be, but GOD certainly does! All you have to do is ask. Its time you get up! Its time you move out! It's time for you to LIVE AGAIN!

Pray for a strategy and do as Mary instructed the people to do when the wine ran out at the wedding in Cana of Galilee. **WHATEVER HE/GOD INSTRUCTS YOU TO DO, DO IT!**

In exercising this new strategy there are several things I learned:

1. When you know you are doing what God said, BE AT PEACE WITH THAT. *(Rest in knowing you are obeying God)*
2. Take your eyes off of others. *(We all can learn from each other, but at the end of the day, ONLY do what GOD told YOU to do)*
3. Be okay if others can't see it. *(God gave it to YOU, don't be disappointed if others can't see what you see)*
4. Only the strategy that you STICK TO will manifest. *(Stay to course until the end)*

CHAPTER 9

EMBRACE ISOLATION

I don't know about anyone else, but often I hear the voice of God. Often times it's very early in the morning in dreams, after awaking and/or lying in bed.

I remember very vividly one morning while lying in bed, I heard these words in my spirit, **"EMBRACE the Cocoon"**. *(This is also the title of a book that I can't wait to write)*

As I begin to meditate on those words, I heard God say clearly to me, **"*if you leave the cocoon before time, you might live a while but you will end up dying without fulfilling your potential. If someone helps you out of the cocoon, they too can kill your potential.*"**

As I pondered these things, I begin to understand that God was telling me to stop begging HIM to get me out of this uncomfortable place. Instead, EMBRACE it because metaphorically, like the caterpillar being developed in its cocoon, God was using this closed, lonely, hurting, and frequently very scary place, to develop something great in me. In the natural, you can remove a caterpillar from its cocoon too soon. It will live and crawl for a while, but die without experiencing the joy of flying as a butterfly.

During my cocoon stage, I came to understand as humans we really struggle more than we are aware of with being isolated and/or alone. Modern technology has made it even more difficult for us to go a few minutes without checking our social media pages, receiving/responding to text messages, or doing something that causes us to not be alone.

Maybe you are experiencing a period in your life where you feel all alone. Perhaps you go out for work or other daily activities and gather there is a deep loneliness in which you feel inside. EMBRACE this place and allow God to do everything He needs to do while you are in this place.

Don't allow the shame, hurt, and pain that you feel to cause you to abandon that place before time. Think of Moses, whose good intentions in trying to save an Egyptian caused Him to be isolated on the back side of the dessert for forty (40) years. Furthermore, when God finally decides to speak, it wasn't about consoling Moses for what he had been through, God was preparing him to be a source in which He would use to deliver his people from over four-hundred (400) years of slavery.

I know you (like I did) want to get out of your situation of isolation. However, know that I've found **I Peter 5:10** to be very true! The scripture reads as follows:

I Peter 5:10 *"And the God of all grace, who called you to his eternal glory in Christ, after you have suffered a little while, will himself restore you and make you strong, firm and steadfast."*

It pains me to even think of the things me and my family suffered as well as lost. With all of what we went through, I can honestly say the rewards of getting to know God, experiencing His supernatural provision, learning my own pressure points, being delivered from people, and all of the other valuable lessons I learned far outweigh the pain and shame that I felt in those moments.

Before I move to the next place, I must add some balance to this place of isolation. ***If you struggle with anxiety or depression, you must be careful that you are not purposely placing yourself in a world of isolation due to this illness. Isolation for an individual who struggles with depression is not good!***

As a person who deals with depression, you should not isolate yourself from people. As matter of fact, you should fight to stay in their midst! Let me tell you, once I embraced my cocoon, I really developed a peace that really surpassed ALL of my understanding. After embracing this place, I begin to do like Paul did when he prayed several times for God to deliver him from the painful thorn in his flesh. I began to allow God's power to be made manifest in that place in my heart. I developed a different perspective of this place of isolation. What I once saw as a place of hurt and shame, I begin to see as a place of preparation. My faith was increased, my spiritual stamina, and my ability to endure became so strong. I moved from a victim mentality to a person who saw everyday life as an opportunity for God to show himself strong in my life.

Understand that the cocoon is not where I was looking die. The cocoon was what I used for development and training. So when the time came for flying, I would be able to gracefully fly as God would have me to do.

I remember listening to a televangelist discussing a time when she was asking God why was she doing ministry in her house, when television, radio, and other ways of getting the

Gospel out was available. She spoke about how she was watching someone who really couldn't preach on television with a worldwide ministry and there she was in her house teaching a bible study. What she came to understand was, although she had a word that could help thousands of people around the world, she didn't have good relationship with her husband. To add, she had several character issues that needed to be worked out. Therefore, she embraced the cocoon and she's now blessing people all over the world!

While you are in this place of hurt, shame and isolation, let God work on you. Allow HIM to adjust whatever needs to be adjusted so when the time comes you will be equipped the fly!

In studying the process of the caterpillar, you will discover that the development and growth stage is what determines the time it will break out of its cocoon and FLY.

I learned to stop whining in that place and use it for personal growth/development. Like the caterpillar, it pushed me out of that place.

NOTE: God placed something within the caterpillar that would enable it to be free to fly! I stopped looking to people or the perfect situation to get me out by realizing everything I needed was in me! God was able to instruct me and the rest is history!

If you are in a place of isolation and dealing with anxiety and/or depression, below are some of things I did when I found myself slipping into that dark place.

NOTE: Although they may not be medically correct, they did wonders for me!

How To Avoid Quitting

FIGHT, FIGHT, FIGHT! The KINGDOM suffers violence, the VIOLENT TAKE IT by FORCE!!! Fight by doing the following:

A. **Worship & Praise God.** The Bible says in **Isaiah 61:3** "The GARMENT of PRAISE will lift the Spirit of HEAVINESS!"
B. **Watch Clean Comedy.** A MERRY HEART doeth good, like Medicine! Do fun things even when you don't feel like it! If you don't like comedy, be intentional by surrounding yourself in an environment that breathes joy, laughter and excitement.
C. **Feed your FAITH.** You are in the faith fight of your life! Listen to faith teachers and preachers! Personally... I don't believe anyone can listen to people like: Earl Dixon Jr. (Shameless Plug) Joyce Myer, Kenneth Copeland, I.V. Hilliard, Dr. Michael D. Moore, and Bill Winston on a REGULAR basis, and stay depressed.
D. **Put NEGATIVE PEOPLE and their DRAMA out of your life!** They will not VOLUNTEER to leave. You HAVE to put them out!
E. **Avoid the FEELING to PURPOSELY ISOLATE yourself from LIFE and PEOPLE!** Isolation needs to be something that just happened due to the situation. Surround yourself with POSITIVE ENCOURAGING PEOPLE!
F. **Refuse and Reject MENTAL LIES!** You, your friends, or life WILL NOT BE BETTER WITHOUT YOU! Put the thought of suicide to rest by committing life! A strong Bible word life will help you in that area. With the WORD of GOD ROOTED in your MIND and SPIRIT, you can CAST DOWN

imaginations and EVERY HIGH THING that exalts itself against the KNOWLEDGE of GOD, thereby bringing these deadly thoughts into Captivity and the OBEDIENCE of CHRIST!

G. Lastly, there is absolutely NOTHING wrong or non-spiritual about having a good encouraging LIFE COACH in your life either! These are ALL the things I did and I'm NOT ASHAMED to share, especially if it helps YOU!

CHAPTER 10

BELIEVE FOR MIRACLES BUT WORK PRINCIPLES

As a believer in Christ, I am unyielding in my belief of the supernatural unseen world. As much I believe in God and His supernatural ability to turn things around in my life, I also learned that miracles are real, they do happen, and God loves extending them to those in need. While I do believe mightily in the supernatural, I discovered in my situation that miracles are fine. But if you desire to come back and remain, you must practice good sound bible principles for living on a regular basis.

Many situations (especially for believers), normally don't call for the supernatural aide of a miracle. In some cases, all that is needed is you practicing some NATURAL principles that will produce positive successful results.

For example, I had a relative who is a minister, visit me while traveling through our city. I allowed him to stay over so he could catch a flight the next day and return home. He proceeded to talk to me of how he once weighed over three-hundred (300) pounds. While living in this state, he said he was taking about five (5) different forms of medication.

Consequently, he got tired of the many health challenges due to being overweight. As a result, he decided to have gastric bypass surgery. He immediately dropped hundreds of pounds and no longer needs any of the medication he was previously taking. My point is this, whether you are in financial trouble or trying to rebound from a tragic life situation, whatever it is that you need to rebound from, it will happen when you make a conscious decision to PRACTICE a principle that will yield the productive fruit that you need.

Often I've heard believers release their faith for supernatural increase. While often times I know God will and have moved for many. However, the other side is simple. The real key to some people's financial trouble is a simple life altering DOWNSIZE! Making a decision to let go of a major house or car payment by moving to a smaller house, apartment or ridding themselves of a vehicle that they couldn't afford from the start. Sure you might damage your credit in process. But you will damage it worst with a repossession or foreclosure!

As a Pastor who believes in the miracle working power of God, I discovered miracles will bring immediate relief to any situation. However, a consistent regiment of practiced principles will sustain you over the long haul. Good principles will also position you to get free of your situation and allow you to become someone else's miracle.

If you are trying to overcome serious financial challenges, God has an inexhaustible supply of resources that can pay all of your bills and have some left over. I mean ALL of them! Mortgage and ALL! But if you violate the principles connected to money like good money management, you will definitely need another miracle in no time!

How To Avoid Quitting

What you should do is seek counsel for whatever area you are looking to overcome. Whatever principles are given that will yield the fruit you are looking to produce, COMMIT to doing them daily. As you practice these principles, you will be amazed of the miracles that God will perform in your situation!

Chapter 11

MAKE UGLY LOOK GOOD

I've had some really nice things said about me over the years! However, one of the greatest things that I've heard to date was when I talked with a pastor concerning all that we had been through. It was his reply that made me the proudest concerning this whole situation. He simply said, "Pastor Dixon… I really didn't know that things were that bad with you, your family or your ministry." In my mind I was thinking how on earth could you not know? From what I had been hearing, people were definitely talking and saying some horrible things. But he said, "every time I saw you and your family, you ALWAYS had a look that said nothing was wrong, you were on your way somewhere, and wherever somewhere was it looked like it was good!"

I cherished those words because I was always taught to go after it. Never look for handouts and never look to present yourself as a person desiring the pity of others. Yes, I used the EBT cards of other people at times. Yes, I've pawned items in local pawn shops. Yes, I've even had my share of title and personal loans. But I do take pride in knowing that we RARELY looked like what we were experiencing!

My mother would often say to me as a child, *"whatever you have or wear, whether it be cheap or of great value, if taken care of properly, it also makes a statement concerning who you are."*

Many nights I feared being evicted. Numerous Sundays I would stand and declare the victory we have in Jesus as if I was in a place of freedom and triumph myself. But the real truth was I took to heart a commercial that use to say, "NEVER LET'EM SEE YOU SWEAT!"

Another thing I learned from my mother was, PRESENTATION is everything and no one is looking to invest in something or someone who appears to be a bad investment. Therefore, regardless of how bad off we were, haircuts, salon visits, and staying presentable was still a LIFESTYLE! It wasn't fake, it wasn't as some say *"fake it until you make it"* either. My family learned to be FIRST CLASS people in our spirits and minds regardless of our hardships!

Where else did this confidence come from? It came from my time in the Word of God. God's Word taught me that my life didn't consist of the abundance of things that I possessed. But my worth and my value is in my character, my integrity, and who GOD says I am in His Word!

We've attended religious galas with no money, but we looked good! There were times when we had dinner knowing beforehand that we ONLY had a certain amount to spend. Nonetheless, we continued to press on. One of the most gratifying places I discovered was like Paul in **Philippians 4:12-13.** *"[12]I know how to be abased, and I know how to abound. Everywhere and in all things I have learned both to be full and to be hungry, both to abound and to suffer need. [13]I can do all things through Christ who strengthens me."*

How To Avoid Quitting

I really should have titled this book "Getting up without the Shame" because another one of my favorite readings is **Isaiah 50:4-9,** *"The Sovereign LORD has given me a well-instructed tongue, to know the word that sustains the weary. He wakens me morning by morning, wakens my ear to listen like one being instructed. ⁵ The Sovereign LORD has opened my ears; I have not been rebellious, I have not turned away. ⁶ I offered my back to those who beat me, my cheeks to those who pulled out my beard; I did not hide my face from mocking and spitting. ⁷ Because the Sovereign LORD helps me, I will not be disgraced.* **Therefore, have I set my face like flint, and I know I will not be put to SHAME** *⁸ He who vindicates me is near. Who then will bring charges against me? Let us face each other! Who is my accuser? Let him confront me! ⁹ It is the Sovereign LORD who helps me. Who will condemn me? They will all wear out like a garment; the moths will eat them up."*

I had many moments where people or situations brought about inward feelings of shame. Continuously, I held on to the word where Isaiah declares HE WOULD NOT LET ME BE MADE ASHAME! It was God's vindication that allowed me to walk in victory. It was God having a man in whom I had never met call me and say, *"I've been looking for you! God told me to find Earl Dixon and find a way to have him lease my building with an option to purchase!"* He held the mortgage until our young ministry was prepared to secure a loan. With less than two (2) years history, three (3) different banks approved our loan. We later purchased that building which appraised for $410,000.00. After closing, we walked away with $40,000.00 to do building improvements and still closed with over $100,000.00 of equity!

Whenever shame tried to set in, God would make one power move after another to validate His hand on our lives and ministry. Even after having a 740 BMW repossessed, a member put the keys in my hand to a FREE, 2009 BMW that we drove for almost two (2) years! Even in the struggle, God used members who worked at airlines to fly my family all over the country at the expense of others. When I thought I was behind on our mortgage, God allowed an ANONYMOUS donor to sow **$9,000.00** towards our mortgage!

Then even after being humiliated by someone who postdated me two (2) checks in the excess of $165,000.00 of which I discovered he had no way of making good on either, I ended up losing on the building project.

After receiving checks, I started declaring budget was met and we'd be remodeling soon. Even then, before Satan could get any glory or the spirit of embarrassment could set in, God gave us favor with a local contractor. The contractor COMPLETELY remodeled our women's restroom for FREE! It was at least a $20,000.00 job!

You can walk with your head up when you don't allow the disappointments of your situation to cloud the hand of God in your life! Right where you are, if you will be honest, you may be in the most difficult place in your life that you've ever imagined. I guarantee if you look carefully, even in that (whatever that may be) you will see GOD is still at work in your life!

But to further explain what I mean by making ugly look good, I'm simply speaking of you not walking or living in such a way that people can either be around you or see you and everything about you says; **STRUGGLE, PAIN, HURT and DISSAPOINTMENT.**

How To Avoid Quitting

Trust me when I tell you, you don't have to fake it either. It's like the three (3) Hebrews boys who the bible says, came out of a burning fiery furnace but looked nothing like what they had been through.

In your struggle let God touch people to help you. Don't drop pity lines in conversation to alarm people to what you are going through. Be careful not to share your hurt and pain in your conversation either.

Please know I'm not suggesting that you internalize all that you are going through. I had several people I could unleash my pain with. I'm speaking of everywhere you go and almost everyone you talk with, you end up sharing all of your pain and disappointment.

I am certain that there are hundreds maybe even thousands of people who will read this book and be totally surprised to hear many of the things I've shared in this book. Why, because I purposed to use my pain to encourage others?

Daily I would use social media outlets to encourage people when many times I needed encouragement myself. No, I wasn't faking! I was simply using the encouragement of others as the healing salve and encouragement for my own heart.

Making ugly look good is suffering like the apostles who counted it an admirable thing to suffer for Christ. Whether you are suffering or enduring a hardness for Christ or other reasons, have some pride in your pain!

I discovered the best way to not be consumed with my own hurt and sorrow was to find ways to get involved in the needs of others. For years I'd wake up praying about how or what I could say to brighten someone else's day opposed to being consumed with my own difficulties. After all, many of my days were days where, if God didn't move or touch someone on my behalf, we would be in trouble!

I have to tell you, in order to do this, **you really have to be spiritual**. Spiritual meaning, you have to have a faith life in God that will give you hope in the midst of anything. Which is another attribute that I humbly thank God for every day. My wife and I were blessed with the ability to put the needs of others above our own many days. I bless God that she is one of the most spiritual persons I know.

Often we would read, pray, worship and do things together that encouraged us until the situations changed. We really learned how to work the word of God in the midst of our disappointments & betrayals.

With that being said, making ugly look good also requires you being faithfully committed to a local church! While I know the church of today is often disrespected for the many human, sinful indiscretions of leaders and local members; the last thing you need to do while suffering any type of life setback is to **BE DISCONNECTED FROM A LOCAL CHURCH!**

Of course being Pastors that is pretty cut and dry for us. But seriously, why do you think I wrote the book? There were times when we've wanted to quit, but our relationship with God, His word, and the local church would not let that be!

As a pastor, I'm amazed of the people who try and endure life challenges and setbacks without God! It's hard as it is WITH God, but doing it without HIM is absolutely absurd!

Whatever you do, stick with your church, and if you don't have one, find one immediately!

How To Avoid Quitting

Before closing this chapter I must reiterate the fact that though the church right now may not be as respected as I, as a pastor, believes it should be; please take my advice and don't attempt to do any part of life without God, the Word or the Local Church being a part of your life!

CHAPTER 12

PRAY FOR A MARY & MARTHA

Out of all of the chapters contained in this book, this chapter is my favorite. This whole idea of Mary and Martha came as a result of me having to deal with a very serious situation that I was facing in my opinion, ALL alone! Then while praying to God, the Holy Spirit led me to one of the most profound bible revelations I know.

John 11:1-3

"11 Now a certain man was sick, named Lazarus, of Bethany, the town of Mary and her sister Martha. 2 (It was that Mary which anointed the Lord with ointment, and wiped his feet with her hair, whose brother Lazarus was sick.) 3 Therefore his sisters sent unto him, saying, Lord, behold, he whom thou lovest is sick. 4 When Jesus heard that, he said, This sickness is not unto death, but for the glory of God, that the Son of God might be glorified thereby. 5 Now Jesus loved Martha, and her sister, and Lazarus. 6 When he had heard therefore that he was sick, he abode two days still in the same place where he was. 7 Then after that saith he to his disciples, Let us go into Judaea again. 8 His disciples say unto him, Master, the Jews of late sought to stone thee; and goest thou thither again? 9 Jesus answered, Are there not twelve hours in the day? If any man walk in the day, he stumbleth not, because he seeth the light of this world. [10] But if a man walk in the night, he stumbleth, because there is no light in him. [11] These things said he: and after that he saith unto them, Our friend Lazarus sleepeth; but I go, that I may awake him out of sleep. [12] Then said his disciples, Lord, if he sleep, he shall do well. [13] Howbeit Jesus spake of his death: but they thought that he had spoken of taking of rest in sleep. [14] Then said Jesus unto them plainly, Lazarus is dead. [15] And I am glad for your sakes that I was not there, to the intent ye may believe; nevertheless let us go unto him. [16] Then said Thomas, which is called Didymus, unto his fellow disciples, Let us also go, that we may die with him. [17] Then when Jesus came, he found that he had lain in the grave four days already. [18] Now Bethany was nigh unto Jerusalem, about fifteen furlongs off: [19] And many of the Jews came to Martha and Mary, to comfort them concerning their brother. [20] Then Martha, as soon as she heard that Jesus was coming, went and met him: but Mary sat still in the house. [21] Then said Martha unto Jesus, Lord, if thou hadst been here, my brother had not died. [22] But I know, that even now, whatsoever thou wilt ask of God, God will give it thee. [23] Jesus saith unto her, Thy brother shall rise again. [24] Martha saith unto him, I know that he shall rise again in the resurrection at the last day. [25] Jesus said unto her, I am the resurrection, and the life: he that believeth in me, though he were dead, yet shall he live: [26] And whosoever liveth and believeth in me shall never die. Believest thou this? [27] She saith unto him, Yea, Lord: I believe that thou art the Christ, the Son of God, which should come into the world. [28] And when she had so said, she went her way, and called Mary her sister secretly, saying, The Master is come, and calleth for thee. [29] As soon as she heard that, she arose quickly, and came unto him. [30] Now Jesus was not yet come into the town, but was in that place where Martha met him. [31] The Jews then which were with her in the house, and comforted her, when they saw Mary, that she rose up hastily and went out, followed her, saying, She goeth unto the grave to weep there. [32] Then when Mary was come where Jesus was, and saw him, she fell down at his feet, saying

How To Avoid Quitting

unto him, Lord, if thou hadst been here, my brother had not died. [33]When Jesus therefore saw her weeping, and the Jews also weeping which came with her, he groaned in the spirit, and was troubled. [34]And said, Where have ye laid him? They said unto him, Lord, come and see. [35]Jesus wept. [36]Then said the Jews, Behold how he loved him! [37]And some of them said, Could not this man, which opened the eyes of the blind, have caused that even this man should not have died? [38]Jesus therefore again groaning in himself cometh to the grave. It was a cave, and a stone lay upon it. [39]Jesus said, Take ye away the stone. Martha, the sister of him that was dead, saith unto him, Lord, by this time he stinketh: for he hath been dead four days. [40]Jesus saith unto her, Said I not unto thee, that, if thou wouldest believe, thou shouldest see the glory of God? [41]Then they took away the stone from the place where the dead was laid. And Jesus lifted up his eyes, and said, Father, I thank thee that thou hast heard me. [42]And I knew that thou hearest me always: but because of the people which stand by I said it, that they may believe that thou hast sent me. [43]And when he thus had spoken, he cried with a loud voice, Lazarus, come forth. [44]And he that was dead came forth, bound hand and foot with graveclothes: and his face was bound about with a napkin. Jesus saith unto them, Loose him, and let him go."

Mary and Martha in this story represent the kind of people you need in your life whether you are rebounding from a life event or not. As I studied this story, the Holy Spirit revealed what I believe should be the kind of people we should have in our inner circles. They are as follows:

1. ***People who are troubled by your illness or setback.*** (Real friends are not ok with you being sick or struggling)
2. ***People who will advocate to Jesus on your behalf.*** (Times when you can seem to pray the right prayer or

do the right thing. You need others who will intercede for you)
3. ***People who have problems with you dying.*** (These are people who are not ok with your demise)
4. ***People who will remove things that are holding you down.*** (These are people ready to move hell on your behalf)
5. ***People who will help you get loose!*** (These are those who will help you gain your freedom. Be leery of people who can soar themselves and watch you be bound)

I'm not suggesting you find people for the sole purpose of helping you. However, I have identified through my experience that you do need people in your life, who fit the description above. If you want to know where people really stand with you, pay attention to their responses when you are in trouble or when things aren't going so good.

One of my greatest disappointments was how many family and friends made it clear that they had either gone as far as they wanted to go me or they concluded that it was many a times my own fault so they were no longer willing to help in what they saw as my own bad behavior!

Oh…not Mary and Martha! These women were the ones who went to Jesus saying, *"He Whom Thou Loves Is Sick"*.

When trying to rebound or get up after a fall or trying not to quit, you need people who can look past what happened and focus on the future potential that they see in you. However, don't be upset with people who you think should help but doesn't. It will however do you good to mark them though!

How To Avoid Quitting

Proverbs 17:17 says, "*A friend loves at all times, and a brother is born for a time of adversity.*"

Maturity has taught me that people aren't bad because they reveal the level of their relationship with you. In your worst days, recognize who clings as well as those who got as far away as possible.

There is a saying that says: **Don't be mad at people for not being there, be mad at yourself for assuming that they would.**

Don't get me wrong, I've had people to do lots of nice things for me, but I'm forever indebted to Bishop Theo Bailey Jr. and Minister Christopher Walker because they had no limitations! They were always there whether I invited them or not! Out of all the people I know, these men went in on my behalf! They showed my family over and over again that they were not okay with our condition and would not be ok until it changed! They refused to let me quit! And believe me when I tell you, there were times when I wanted to throw it all in!

Also the members of my current church, they continued to show up week after week, encouraging me as I sought to lead and encourage them.

But notice how Mary and Martha interceded on Lazarus behalf. Value and appreciate those in your life who will pray and talk to God on your behalf! The last thing you need when trying not to quit or to recover is someone in your life who's more concern with how you went down, than what you are going to do to get up!

You see, Mary and Martha had an issue with Lazarus getting sick. People in your life that are ok with you being sick, are not the type of people you need in your inner circle!

Again, allow me to emphasize that those who are ok are not always an enemy. They are simply not the ones you should choose as inner circle people! Dr. Mike Murdock says: when people reveal who they are believe them.

Today I still have lots of good people involved in my life. Many are just not people who I look to in times of need.

What I love about this story is, nowhere does the bible speak of is Lazarus doing hardly anything. It was the intercession, the concerns and willingness of Mary & Martha as they followed Jesus' instructions that made a world of difference!

Now allow me to make this clear! I am not suggesting that you only look for people to help bail you out every time you get involved in anything. However, at the same time I am suggesting that be careful who the people that you position in your life as ride or dies or inner circle people.

I believe this from my own experience; all of us at one time or another will go through or experience a place in our lives where the aide of our close relatives or friends will be detrimental us overcoming situations in life.

Knowing this, it would be wise to make sure you have at least two people who aren't ok with your mishaps, setbacks and or struggles in life.

I can recall times when I felt totally dejected. While many had the attitude that said good for you, these two guys would speak life into me like I've never experienced before.

Also many of times the congregation that I Pastor. Although small in number, Kingdom Ministries have been a blessing in my life!

How To Avoid Quitting

I remember this one occasion, when I was about ready to quit, I was in the car with Chris and with tears in my eyes, I expressed how tired I was with everything I was dealing with. He looks back at me in the spirit of laughter saying: Man if you could see what God showed me about you! He proceeded to tell me several things he saw concerning a situation we were dealing with concerning our bank and our church. Not many days from that time God did to the very letter EVERYTHING that he described in the car that day.

Maybe you are reading this, and you are saying well good for you. And you don't feel you have anyone. Well, I'm praying that even as you read this book, God is placing a few people in your path to help minister and encourage you to stay your course. But another important thing that have to be addressed is: have you lived or made way for such people to come into your life?

I discovered alone the way that some people are so independent that others aren't welcomed into their situation. There is a saying that I found to be true that says: **No man is an island, no man stands alone!** Regardless of who you are, there are some things that we will experience that will require the need of others.

In closing this chapter, please allow me to advise you! Whatever you did, use integrity! Don't use good people just because you know they are available. But also welcome them when they do appear!

CHAPTER 13

MAKE REST A PRIORITY

Jesus said in in **Matthew 11:28**, "Come to me, all you who are weary and burdened, and I will give you rest. In **Mark 6:31**, Jesus instructed His disciples to go into a dessert place and rest, "³¹Then, because so many people were coming and going that they did not even have a chance to eat, he said to them, 'Come with me by yourselves to **a** quiet **place and** get some **rest.**'"

There is value in REST and RELAXATION! Whether you are seeking to rebound from a terrible divorce, a stressful financial situation or any form of traumatic life event that has you feeling like you are at a place of no return, it is a must that you fight to maintain and LIVE in a dwelling of rest!

The Hebrew writer speaks of a rest for the people of God, but we must labor to enter therein! **Hebrews 4:9-11** states, "9 There remaineth therefore a rest to the people of God. ¹⁰For he that is entered into his rest, he also hath ceased from his own works, as God did from his. ¹¹Let us labor therefore to enter into that rest, lest any man fall after the same example of unbelief."

I've come to understand in the midst of some of my most adverse conditions that REST that consist of lying on a bed/couch, with a remote control in your hand, and no cares in this world, are essential to the restoration of your mind, body, and soul!

Rest is also a way of thinking. Rest is a mindset that allows one to remain cool, calm and collected when all things around them are in a state of turmoil! Rest is you in the fire, KNOWING and believing just like the Hebrew boys, that Jesus is in the midst! It's been said that God expects us to remain firm and calm in our faith. Honestly, my internal fire was so hot, I was anything but calm during my difficult times.

One day while meeting with my pastor, this revelation came to my mind. I had discussed with him how there was no more fight left in me and I was ready to shut the ministry down. It was then that Pastor Timothy Woods said, *"Earl you are a good preacher. Man… you don't want to do that, you are just tired from the battle."*

He then told me how I had already won, but was fatigued from the day to day struggles of this trying time in my life. That's when God revealed to me what happens when we get physically tired from life's battles. Pastor Woods, being the bible man that he is, led me to the story of the prophet Elijah. It was when the prophet Elijah got tired and ran away from Jezebel, after defeating the four-hundred fifty (450) prophets of Baal on Mount Carmel.

I don't desire to PREACH here, please read the following verses. As you read, there are 4 things that Pastor Woods showed me concerning this story. This I believe was due to

How To Avoid Quitting

Elijah being physically drained from the previous battle he had fought.

I Kings 19:1-16 states, *"And Ahab told Jezebel all that Elijah had done, and withal how he had slain all the prophets with the sword. ²Then Jezebel sent a messenger unto Elijah, saying, so let the gods do to me, and more also, if I make not thy life as the life of one of them by tomorrow about this time. ³And when he saw that, he arose, and went for his life, and came to Beersheba, which belongeth to Judah, and left his servant there. ⁴But he himself went a day's journey into the wilderness, and came and sat down under a juniper tree: and he requested for himself that he might die; and said, it is enough; now, O LORD, take away my life; for I am not better than my fathers. ⁵And as he lay and slept under a juniper tree, behold, then an angel touched him, and said unto him, arise and eat. ⁶And he looked, and, behold, there was a cake baken on the coals, and a cruse of water at his head. And he did eat and drink, and laid him down again. ⁷And the angel of the LORD came again the second time, and touched him, and said, Arise and eat; because the journey is too great for thee. ⁸And he arose, and did eat and drink, and went in the strength of that meat forty days and forty nights unto Horeb the mount of God. ⁹And he came thither unto a cave, and lodged there; and, behold, the word of the LORD came to him, and he said unto him, What doest thou here, Elijah? ¹⁰And he said, I have been very jealous for the LORD God of hosts: for the children of Israel have forsaken thy covenant, thrown down thine altars, and slain thy prophets with the sword; and I, even I only, am left; and they seek my life, to take it away. ¹¹And he said, Go forth, and stand upon the mount before the LORD. And, behold, the LORD passed by, and a great and strong wind rent the mountains, and brake in pieces the rocks before the LORD; but the LORD was not in the wind: and after the wind an earthquake; but the LORD was not in the earthquake: ¹²And after the earthquake a fire; but the LORD was not in the fire: and after the fire a still small voice. ¹³And it was so, when Elijah heard it, that* *he wrapped his face in his mantle, and went out, and stood in the entering in of the cave. And, behold, there came a voice unto him, and said, What doest thou here, Elijah? ¹⁴And he said, I have been very jealous for the* LORD *God of hosts: because the children of Israel have forsaken thy covenant, thrown down thine altars, and slain thy prophets with the sword; and I, even I only, am left; and they seek my life, to take it away. ¹⁵And the* LORD *said unto him, Go, return on thy way to the wilderness of Damascus: and when thou comest, anoint Hazael to be king over Syria: ¹⁶And Jehu the son of Nimshi shalt thou anoint to be king over Israel: and Elisha the son of Shaphat of Abelmeholah shalt thou anoint to be prophet in thy room."*

You see, when you are physically and/or spiritually tired several things will happen:

1. **You start running from things you use to fight and defeat** (Just defeats four-hundred fifty (450) prophets now he's running from a woman)!
2. **You starting making moves you shouldn't make** (Now he's traveled to a place that God did not instruct him to go).
3. **You start speaking things that you really don't mean.** (He asked God to take his life)!
4. **You start speaking doubt and disbelief.** (Now he's saying he's not better than his fathers)

It's amazing that this man in one chapter went as far as to mock and taunt his opposition by saying in **I Kings 18:4**, *"²⁷And it came to pass at noon, that Elijah mocked them, and said, Cry aloud: for he is a god; either he is talking, or he is pursuing, or he is in a journey, or peradventure he sleepeth, and must be awaked."* Then in verse three (3) he's running for his life due to a threat from Jezebel. Did he forget the SUPERNATURAL power of GOD, who sent fire from heaven and could have also

How To Avoid Quitting

handled Jezebel too? Now in fear of his life, he disobeys God's instructions, opens his mouth, and utters a suicidal desire to die!

I Kings 19:4 *" ⁴But he himself went a day's journey into the wilderness, and came and sat down under a juniper tree: and he requested for himself that he might die; and said, It is enough; now, O LORD, take away my life; for I am not better than my fathers."*

Pastor Woods concluded our conversation by saying, "You know he didn't mean this. If he really wanted to die, all he had to do was stop running and Jezebel would have handled that." As tired as I was and as much as I felt like I wanted to quit, quitting alone probably would've killed me. I was born for what I do! When you are tired and frustrated, you will say things you really don't mean.

This is why I believe you should train your mouth. Our words are powerful. Death and life are in the power of the tongue!

Looking back on it all, I thank God I didn't quit. Before I got this revelation I had a mouth full of doom! Saying words like, *"I'm so tired… Lord why? Jesus this doesn't make any sense! I'm sick of this or sick of that!"* My tongue became the tongue of a tired quitter!

I've always been the type of person who acts quickly. Once I left Pastor Woods, I immediately organized and scheduled a get-away to simply rest. My wife and I rented a vehicle, took less than a $1,000.00 and drove to Columbus, Ohio to visit her sister. From there we traveled to Granger, Indiana to visit my sister. Later, we drove over to Chicago, Illinois to a family reunion where I met family on my father's side and saw for the very first time. The plan was just to get away from all of the chaos we were facing!

Remember, rest is a state of mind. It's the ability to be cool, calm, and collected in the midst of chaos. This is the beginning to developing a peaceful mindset. Rest, I believe, also comes with a REAL REVELATION of who GOD is and what He is to you.

The Psalmist said in **Psalm 46** New International Version:

*Psalm 46:**1-11**, "**1** God is our refuge and strength, an ever-present help in trouble. **2**Therefore we will not fear, though the earth give way and the mountains fall into the heart of the sea, **3**though its waters roar and foam and the mountains quake with their surging. **4**There is a river whose streams make glad the city of God, the holy place where the Most High dwells. **5**God is within her, she will not fall; God will help her at break of day. **6**Nations are in uproar, kingdoms fall; he lifts his voice, the earth melts. **7**The Lord Almighty is with us; the God of Jacob is our fortress. **8**Come and see what the Lord has done, the desolations he has brought on the earth. **9**He makes wars cease to the ends of the earth. He breaks the bow and shatters the spear; he burns the shields with fire. **10**He says, "Be still, and know that I am God; I will be exalted among the nations, I will be exalted in the earth." **11**The Lord Almighty is with us; the God of Jacob is our fortress."*

The Psalmist is clear on several things. He knows for certain that God will be there in times of trouble. Likewise, through our personal relationships with God, we must recognize that our heavenly Father is with us. God cares for us and He will always be there in a time of need, REGARDLESS!

The bible is full of promises that assures us that GOD will not allow the sorrows of this world to take us out. We have to BELIEVE that every word is true.

How To Avoid Quitting

Each time the angel of the Lord appeared to Elijah, his instructions were to arise and eat. **I Kings 19:7**, *"And the angel of the LORD came again the second time, and touched him, and said, Arise and eat; because the journey is too great for thee."* You may not be able to take a trip like we did, but you must do whatever you can to physically rest.

Whenever, couples visit my office for counselling, one of the first things I suggest is a get-away. I suggest this because a tired mental state is nothing to take lightly. Remember when Jesus asked His disciple to go away and pray with Him for one hour? They couldn't do that which was spiritual because they were too tired physically.

Perhaps this is why it's so hard for people to really believe the promises of God in regards to daily living.

Could it be that you are too tired physically that you can't focus long enough to receive that which is spiritual? As the angel said to Elijah, I say to you; ARISE, EAT and DRINK. As bad as things may be in your life right now, you might need a PHYSICAL REFRESHING FIRST!

Whatever you do, choose to get some REST!

Very few people get adequate rest. Often times when you ask a person why he or she isn't resting as they should, the answer is, *"I'm too busy to rest."* Trust me when I tell you, you'd be amazed at the renewed perspective a restful mind would reveal versus those who would typically fold in situations, due to a lack thereof.

Make rest a priority! Remember, rest is more of a mindset than it is sitting or lying in a room, while watching your favorite show. Rest takes place when you learn to train your thought life.

Philippians 4:8 says, *"⁸ Finally, brethren, whatsoever things are true, whatsoever things are honest, whatsoever things are just, whatsoever things are pure, whatsoever things are lovely, whatsoever things are of good report; if there be any virtue, and if there be any praise, think on these things."*

In training your thoughts you must exercise and understand that it requires just that, TRAINING. For whatever reason, I've discovered most people first instinct is to focus on what went wrong or what isn't right. Contrary to what popular belief says, POSITIVE THINKING is very powerful!

Powerful it is, but easy it is not! You must make intentional and deliberate efforts to think positive. Training your thoughts to see the good in things over the bad is amazingly restful! The Hebrew writer says, *"We must LABOR to enter into that place of rest in God."*

In laboring, we must be careful of what we meditate on, what we hear, and the environments that we frequent. We must make others around us aware that we are working to be positive and allow them to hold us accountable when we're being negative.

Although it requires work, the benefits are so rewarding. I often tell my wife how amazed I am about how we handled things. After getting back in faith and operating in the things outlined in the book, one day I commended my wife for how well we both begin the handle the hardships we faced. I knew people were saying ugly things about me, but it was as if I didn't even hear them towards the end.

How To Avoid Quitting

Regardless of what blow life has dealt you, I believe if you will fortify your mind with the Word of God, you will look at the oppositions of life so much more differently than before. Mental rest is essential and it starts with you resting physically.

Earl Dixon

CHAPTER 14

PUT YOUR DEVELOPMENT OVER YOUR REPUTATION

"You are failing in learning some valuable life lessons because you are paying more attention to how people see you, than what's being developed in you in the midst of your trial!"

In fifty-five (55) years of life I've heard much. Yet another one of the most powerful statements I've heard, was in listening to one of the most respected Pastors I know, Dr. Willie B. O'Neal. While listening to Dr. O'Neal one day I heard these words: **"You are failing in learning some valuable life lessons because you are paying more attention to how people see you, than what's being developed in you in the midst of your trial!"**

I was riding alone during the holiday season and talking out loud to God. My conversation with God was concerning me doing what I had desired to do for my family at that time. I was telling God how unfair all of this was and how there were people doing far worse than what I was accused of and appeared to be living life to the fullest. I was like the Pharisee in **Luke 18:10-14,** "*₁₀ "Two men went up to the temple to pray, one a*

Pharisee and the other a tax collector. ¹¹*The Pharisee stood by himself and prayed: 'God, I thank you that I am not like other people—robbers, evildoers, adulterers—or even like this tax collector.* ¹²*I fast twice a week and give a tenth of all I get.'* ¹³*"But the tax collector stood at a distance. He would not even look up to heaven, but beat his breast and said, 'God, have mercy on me, a sinner.'* ¹⁴*"I tell you that this man, rather than the other, went home justified before God. For all those who exalt themselves will be humbled, and those who humble themselves will be exalted."*

After this long EMOTIONAL spill to God in prayer, I heard with clarity the Holy Spirit say these words to me, "Are your concerns REALLY about YOU or more about HOW you are being seen in your family and by people who know a little about what's happening with you?" I felt such a conviction in my heart. I KNEW the Holy Spirit wasn't asking this question because He wanted to know the answer. I KNEW it was because His AWESOME love for me to be developed and grow, had just shined a light on a problem that lied deep within me.

I heard the phrase "You Need to Be Delivered from People" for years. What I thought was truth wasn't and it was at that moment I discovered an even greater freedom. I was able to be honest with myself and God by expressing that most of the frustration, pain, embarrassment I was experiencing wasn't ALL about the trauma of what was happening. Although traumatic experiences played a major role, It really was more about what I thought people were saying.

Boy was I relieved! Once I admitted it, I begin to be free in this:

1. The very people I was concerned over showed me NONE!

How To Avoid Quitting

2. The very people I didn't want to know, didn't CARE about me anyway.
3. The very people I spent years trying to impress either cared less or were such haters that they would never give me credit regardless of what I did.

When I did that, my eyes became open to things that I did to contribute to the whole situation. Although I know God didn't orchestrate this, He did allow it. That's when I started saying to God, "Lord while I'm here, please reveal in and to me everything I need, so I can come out of this wiser, stronger, and better." Like the caterpillar in the dark tight cocoon, I want to come out of this flying!

That's when my PERSONAL DEVLOPMENT begin to outweigh everything. Some of what I learned is as follows:

- **How to wait without whining.**
- **How not express everything I FEEL.** (Trust me, I don't share it all)
- **Accepting criticism whether fair or unfair.** (People talk regardless)
- **How to FOCUS for real!**
- **God's idea of forgiveness.** (God knew all of it before it happened. He STILL called me!)
- **How much GOD loved me in spite of everything!**

Of course, there were and still are many other lessons I've learned. Just being able to practice personal development, proved to be very rewarding.

Now as I look back, I see many days of frustration and anguish could have been avoided, by simply placing more emphasis on lessons, instead of what I could have done to save face! Whatever situation you are trying to get up from, at least be honest enough to ask yourself questions like the following:

1. Could this have been avoided?
2. Was I responsible in any way for this?
3. What can I learn from it?

I close this chapter with these words: STOP TRYING TO SAVE FACE AND LEARN FROM IT! WHATEVER YOUR IT IS!

SPECIAL NOTE: A lot of my problems eventually lead to major financial challenges that created the stress and anxiety I experienced. Below are some things that I highly recommend if your issues are the same:
HELPFUL HINTS for Financial Dilemmas

- **AVOID at ALL COST payday advance loans.**

- **AVOID at ALL COST pawning your valuables due to the pressure!**

- **RELY on PROVEN RELATIONSHIPS, ONLY TRUST AND DEPEND on GOD!**

- **AVOID at ALL COST borrowing money from friends or family. You can run the risk of damaging good relationships!**

- Be willing to **LOSE** instead of getting quick fixes! Often times God desires to help you, only if you will stop trying to help Him.

How To Avoid Quitting

- Don't expect **FAMILY** or **FRIENDS** to volunteer to help you! You will discover in tough times who's really on your team.

- **BE BRUTALLY** honest concerning the part you played in the situation.

- **EXPECT** the **WRONG PEOPLE** to leave you or withdraw from you!

- **NEVER** look for your help to come from people you've helped! Remember, you reap **WHAT** you sow, not **WHERE!**

- Get as much financial information as possible! Be willing to let someone teach you in this area.

- Pray for God to deal with your heart in your process. It will be just like God to make you Bless the very people who watched you squirm.

CHAPTER 15

FORGIVE

Matthew 6:14-15 *14For if ye forgive men their trespasses, your heavenly Father will also forgive you: 15But if ye forgive not men their trespasses, neither will your Father forgive your trespasses.*

I saved this chapter for last on purpose. Why? Because as angry as I was with many people, (Believe me I was ANGRY) forgiveness has been a strength for me due to a simple revelation I received years ago reading **Matthew 6:14-15**.

In my opinion, if you have any good qualities in your life and can read with understanding, FORGIVENESS is very cut and dry.

The Bible says: *If you can't forgive men/people, then GOD can't and won't forgive you!*

Regardless of what anyone said, did or didn't do, I understood that prior to any offense that others may have caused me, I've been guilty of lots of things that required the forgiveness of God towards me. I knew if God was going to be graceful and merciful to me, then I had to extend the same to others.

For years, as a child without this revelation, I was very angry with my biological father who wasn't that much a part of my life growing up. I literally hated him for not being an active part of my life. But once I read **Matthew 6:14-15**, I knew I had to forgive him as well.

Another one of my qualities is: I'm BRUTALLY honest with myself! What I mean by this is: I really work hard on not lying to myself about anything I do. Good or bad, I really am my own worst critic! Again, I understood that in 55 years of life, I've done many things to others as well as to my own self that required God's forgiveness towards me. And if I expect God to forgive me, then I needed to find a way to forgive others.

As it relate to the many things outlined in this book, as hurt, bitter, disappointed and often downright upset I was, my motivation came easy because of the assignment on my life in the midst of all the chaos.

During this time, my wife and 3 young children didn't have the same perspective as I did in this area. They were devastatingly hurt and disappointed on many levels. As a Pastor of this new and fresh ministry, I had to literally show them how to love and forgive people in-spite of their evils.

Believe me when I tell you they were angry! Often times, my advice to them was: Come on guys, we can't allow the hurt and pain we now feel to cause us to no longer trust and serve God's people! We have a current assignment that has nothing to do with the past. We can't make the good people in our lives today, pay for what others did in the past.

How To Avoid Quitting

Imagine a wife and her children often watching her husband and their dad do all kinds of things to help others, and many of the very people who he helped and assisted the most, do very ugly things to hurt and assassinate the life and character of their love one?

As I said at the beginning of this book, my focus is not to rehash or attempt to tell my side of an ugly story. My focus is what God did to get us through. I could write chapters in depth of things my family suffered at the hands of many. But that's not important!

What's important is: With God's help, I was able to minister healing to them as a result of my own ability to release and forgive too.

Maybe you are reading this and your story is on a completely different level than mine. Maybe yours is so excruciatingly different that even as you are reading, your thoughts are: **"THERES NO WAY IM LETTING MY OFFENDER/OFFENDERS** *off the hook by forgiving them!* Your exact thoughts are: Pastor, YOU HAVE NO CLUE OF WHAT HAPPENED TO ME!

Well my response to you is: NO I don't! And there is no way I would insult the legitimacy of what you went through by being insensitive to the reality of it or the depth of the pain it caused.

I will say this though, I also discovered it is true when you hear people say that forgiveness is about YOU and that it helps YOU!

After many years of being bitterly unforgiving to my father. I decided I'm saved, I'm in God and it's time I at least need to talk to my dad concerning the anger and resentment that I had towards him. And honestly speaking, I met with him expecting an apology. On the contrary, I got the total opposite of what I was expecting. After meeting with him I prayed in my car saying something like: God I released him! And he didn't even say he was sorry or acted apologetic at all for the lack of parental involvement in my life!

God's answer to me was: None of this was about him! It was about you releasing the ugly unforgiving feelings out of your heart!

Then God said: ***"You cannot perfect my agape love in an UNFORGIVING heart! If you are going to grow and be successful in my agape love, FORGIVENESS is a MUST! A heart that HARBORS UNFORGIVENESS WILL NEVER be able to TRULY LOVE!"***

In being totally honest with myself and my family, I had to first forgive myself because; regardless of what I felt others did or didn't do, I had to admit to the part I played in our setbacks as well.

Truth is, had I followed the advice of my Pastor at the time, things could have been a lot different. So I assumed responsibility of my role as well as the role of others. In doing so, I was able allow the LOVE of God to grow larger than my anger which gave me an even greater ability to forgive.

Whether you have a legitimate right to be angry, hurt and disappointed, allow the love of God to become perfected in your own heart by releasing your offender by faith!

I say this because, there are situations where forgiveness must be a matter of faith.

How To Avoid Quitting

Remember when Jesus told His disciples in **Luke 17:3-5** that they had to forgive seventy times seven? The disciple's response was: ***LORD increase our Faith!*** They knew to forgive in the manner that Jesus instructed would require a power greater than themselves.

Luke 17:3-5 *Take heed to yourselves: If thy brother trespass against thee, rebuke him; and if he repent, forgive him. 4 And if he trespass against thee seven times in a day, and seven times in a day turn again to thee, saying, I repent; thou shalt forgive him. 5 And the apostles said unto the Lord, Increase our faith.*

In your case, knowing you will need God's forgiveness may not be what it meant for me. However, you need to know that forgiveness is a real key to overcoming hurt and disappointment caused by others.

For me it was recognizing that I myself am human and still often come up short in my walk with God. ***And if I want God to forgive me freely, then I must do the same according to His word with others!***

FREE your own heart by forgiving!

APPENDIX

THE ANSWER SHEET: STARTER KIT

I reiterate that the Word of God is the *Answer*. The following is a template of scripture reference to muse upon, mediate on, ruminate (redundancy intentional) and actively allow it to become a part of your spirit as you hide God's Word in your heart.

These topics are discussed in this book. It is my hope that these scriptures can be a catalyst to give you a head start in combating the issues of life with the offensive weaponry of the Word of God. Please strengthen yourself in the Word by adding more scripture as the Word ministers to your situation.

Back In Faith

- **Mark 9:24** *"And straightway the father of the child cried out, and said with tears, Lord I believe; help thou mine unbelief."*
- **Romans 10:17** *"So then faith cometh by hearing, and hearing by the word of God."*

- **Romans 10:14 ESV** *"How then will they call on him in whom they have not believed? And how are they to believe in him of whom they have never heard? And how are they to hear without someone preaching?"*
- **Hebrews 11:6** *"But without faith* it is *impossible to please* him: *for he that cometh to God must believe that he is, and* that *he is a rewarder of them that diligently seek him."*
- **Mark 11:24** *"Therefore I tell you, whatever you ask for in prayer, believe that you have received it, and it will be yours."*

Bitterness

- **Ephesians 4:31, 32** *"Let all bitterness and wrath and anger and clamor and slander be put away from you, along with all malice. Be kind to one another, tenderhearted, forgiving each other, just as God in Christ also has forgiven you."*

Believing for Miracles

- **Psalms 27:13** *"I had fainted, unless I had believed to see the goodness of the Lord in the land of the living"*

Embracing Your Isolated Period

- ***I Peter 5:10*** *"And the God of all grace, who called you to his eternal glory in Christ, after you have suffered a little while, <u>will himself restore you and make you strong, firm and steadfast.</u>"*

Entitlement

- **James 4:6** *"But he gives more grace. Therefore it says, 'God opposes the proud, but gives grace to the humble.'"*

How To Avoid Quitting

Financial Hardship

- **Philippians 4:19** *"But my God shall supply all your need according to his riches in glory by Christ Jesus.""*

Mental Health

- **Philippians 2:5** *"Let this mind be in you, which is also in Christ Jesus:"*

New Strategy

- **James 1:5** *"If any of you lack wisdom, let him ask of God, that giveth to all men liberally, and upbraideth not; and it shall be given him."*

Personal Development

- **2 Timothy 2:15** *"<u>Study</u> to shew thyself approved unto God, a workman that needeth not to be ashamed, rightly dividing the word of truth."*

Reputation

- **Philippians 2:7** *"But made himself of no reputation, and took upon him the form of a servant and was made in the likeness of men:"*

Rest

- **Hebrews 4:11** *"Let us labour therefore to enter into that rest, lest any man fall after the same example of unbelief."*
- **Mark 6:31** *"Then, because so many people were coming and going that they did not even have a chance to eat, he said to them, 'Come with me by yourselves to a quiet place and get some rest.'"*

Standing on God's Word

- ***Psalm 119:46-52*** *"Remember the word to Your servant, Upon which You have caused me to hope. ⁵⁰ This is my comfort in my affliction, For Your word has given me life. ⁵¹ The proud have me in great derision, Yet I do not turn aside from Your law. ⁵² I remembered Your judgments of old, O LORD, And have comforted myself."*

- **Hebrews 10:35** *"Cast not away therefore your confidence, which hat great recompense of reward."*

Suicide

- **Psalms 34:18-19** *"The Lord is near to the brokenhearted and saves the crushed in spirit. Many are the afflictions of the righteous, but the Lord delivers him out of them all."*

- **Psalms 55:22** *"Cast your burden on the Lord and he will sustain you, he will never permit the righteous to be moved."*

- **Joshua 1:9** *"Have I not commanded you? Be strong and courageous. Do not be frightened, and do not be dismayed, for the Lord your God is with you wherever you go".*

UGLY Looks Good

- **1 Peter 4:12-19 Message (MSG)** *¹²⁻¹³ Friends, when life gets really difficult, don't jump to the conclusion that God isn't on the job. Instead, be glad that you are in the very thick of what Christ experienced. This is a spiritual refining process, with glory just around the corner. ¹⁴⁻¹⁶ If you are abused because of Christ, count yourself fortunate. It's the Spirit of God and his glory in you that brought you to the notice of others. If they're on you because you broke the law or disturbed the peace, that's a different matter. But if it's because you are a Christian, don't*

How To Avoid Quitting

give it a second thought. Be proud of the distinguished status reflected in that name!"

Appendix Kim Davis Williams

ABOUT THE AUTHOR

After 14 years of pastoring, Pastor Earl Dixon Jr. obeyed the voice of God in planting Life Changers Ministries International. During that time God blessed Life Changers to bless the lives of many people.

However, after 11 years of successful ministry under the name Life Changers, being INFUSED with the Gospel message of the KINGDOM of God, Life Changers changed its name to KINGDOM MINISTRIES!

Pastor Earl Dixon's uncompromising, bold and upfront teaching has led to many amazing accomplishments.

He is a religious author with 4 books to his credit entitled: "Pastoral Abuse, The Other Side of the Story", "How To Handle Your Creditors", "Understanding the Processing of God" & "Maximizing Your Membership".

Husband to Co-Pastor Pamela Ann Dixon; father of three children: Ashley Nicole, Gabriel Maurice, Jonathan Earl and grandfather to Terrence Lamar Epps.

Once asked how he characterizes his assignment in the kingdom of God, Pastor Dixon's response was: "I see myself as one who Motivate and Provokes Change."

His assignment at Kingdom Ministries is to EMPOWER PEOPLE WITH THE MESSAGE OF THE KINGDOM!

Learn more about Pastor Earl Dixon Jr.

http://www.edjministries.org/

www.ingramcontent.com/pod-product-compliance
Lightning Source LLC
Chambersburg PA
CBHW070925160426
43193CB00011B/1578